MW01115107

Glimpses of Happi[ness]
time capsules remin[d]
as a society riding a
the information age

and regardless of how our lives and those around us change, some basic emotions and rites of passage will always be the same. Thank you Jerome Perlmutter for capturing bits of Americana from our past, so that we can see the connections to our future.

Paul Kozakiewicz
Journalist and former newspaper publisher

Glimpses of Happiness make me wish I could have known the author personally. His warmth, intelligence and humor shine through in each and every word.

Heidi Swillinger
San Francisco Bay Area journalist and book editor

Glimpses of Happiness was written by an observer of life's foibles and lovingly brought to us by his daughter, Diane Perlmutter Reynolds. It is as though Jerome H. Perlmutter resides in the part of our brains that looks at situations and agrees with us about the absurdity or bittersweet nature of what we share. His coverage of a myriad of everyday topics will leave you with stronger cheek muscles, because you will be smiling throughout this book.

Roberta Schultz Benor
Author and Lecturer

Glimpses Of Happiness

Laughter for the Soul

Glimpses Of
Happiness

Laughter for the Soul

Dear Perlmutter Reynolds

JEROME H. PERLMUTTER

WITH DIANE PERLMUTTER REYNOLDS

AUTHORSOURCE
MEDIA

Glimpses Of Happiness

Laughter for the Soul

Published by AuthorSource Media
www.AuthorSourceMedia.com

ISBN: 978-1-947939-43-1
Printed in the United States of America

Glimpses of Happiness is dedicated to Evelyn Perlmutter. Loving wife and partner of 57 years.

Glimpses of Happiness
_ In his own words

National Endowment for the Arts – Bicentennial Celebration

Glimpses of Happiness is a compendium of description of life's foibles that play out at home, in the office, at movies, theaters, arenas, in streets, and on highways and byways.

Read a Glimpse and it will reveal familiar places and the people who live there, doctors, dentists, lawyers, businessmen, family members, babies, friends, adversaries, mentors, and travelers.

You will find the Glimpses are occasionally serious, but most are humorous and whimsical. Accept this caveat: I do not wish to offend. I have deep respect and an abiding faith in America's healers and helpers.

My approach is simple. With each Glimpse, I visualize YOU. You might say, "It can happen and it does." I hope you do.

Enjoy these *Glimpses of Happiness!*

Jerome H. Perlmutter

Introducing
Jerome H. Perlmutter
—A daughter's remembrance

My father, Jerome Perlmutter, wrote *Glimpses of Happiness* during his fourteen year battle with a brain tumor.

He was a writer, editor, teacher, communicator, and a father of three. From his early years he always carried a small spiral notebook in his pocket so he could jot down ideas and random musings.

A Phi Beta Kappa graduate of George Washington University, he earned his master's degree at American University in 1955. On his professional path, he served in positions both in the private sector and in government, including posts at the National Education Association, the Department of Agriculture, and the Department of State. He later worked with Nancy Hanks at the National Endowment for the Arts and taught writing and editing at the World Bank.

"Retirement" was not a word that was easy for Jerry to consider. At an age many would consider doing just that, he went out on his own, launching Perlmutter Associates, a communications firm, where he consulted and collaborated with top experts in Washington, D.C., and abroad.

In 1963, he was honored as one of ten outstanding men in federal service under forty years of age and received the Arthur S. Fleming award. He authored *A Practical Guide to Effective Writing,* published by Random House in 1965 and used it as a textbook for the many years he taught writing and editing throughout the D.C. area and beyond.

In 1991, Jerry was diagnosed with a brain tumor. Although benign, the tumor was invasive and introduced a long illness that took his life in 2005. Having spent many years as a wordsmith, he turned to writing in a personal way when the tumor was diagnosed. It became not only his therapy but also a way to immerse himself in something that enabled him to retain his dignity, pride and, most importantly, his infectious sense of humor. By the time he passed away on October 6th, he had written more than 500 snippets about everyday life—the basis of *Glimpses of Happiness.*

Glimpses of Happiness is to honor my Dad, Jerome H. Perlmutter. In doing so, I have published a book of his best writings in hopes that it will serve as an inspiration and source of humor, adding something light and whimsical to everyday life experiences.

Enjoy....

Diane Perlmutter Reynolds

Contents

CLOTHING & FASHION

COMMENTARIES

Commerce & Money

Communication - Reading, Writing, Listening, Speaking

DINING & FOOD

EVERYDAY LIFE

FAMILIES - BABIES, KIDS, & CHILDREN

MEDICAL

PETS & OTHER ANIMALS

SITUATIONS & EVENTS

SOCIALIZING

SPORTS & RECREATION

TRAVEL & TRANSPORTATION

WEATHER

Glimpses Of Happiness

Laughter for the Soul

Art & Entertainment

Abstract Art

On the walls of art galleries throughout the world hang abstract paintings that interest viewers who seem intent in deriving the full benefits that the paintings can offer. Facial expressions are revealing. At a New York gallery, husband and wife look perplexed. The Louvre in Paris accommodates several head-scratchers. The Prado in Madrid is the scene of a student field trip. "What is that?" a student asks. The teacher replies with confidence and authority, "THE STATUE OF LIBERTY." Using their native language, all students shout in unison, "Nada." The teacher: "The artist sees the subject and interprets to convey image and design. It's his rendition of what the statue should look like. That's abstract art." Noting that the vast majority has their doubts, teacher indicates the subject will serve as a basis for class discussion.

At the Ballet

Refusenick ballet dancers pose serious problems for producer, director, musicians, and audience waiting for the house lights to dim, overture down beat, and curtains to part revealing a French city during the revolution with flags and bunting. Dancers punctuate the scene as they glide on stage from side holding rooms. Encouraging applause and shouts. Performers respond with waves and deep bows. The program begins, but patrons of the arts detect serious glitches. The prima ballerina forgoes dancing on her toes and becomes flat footed. Why? "Is she ill?" asks some. "No, she's tired," answers others. "Then let her seek another line of work." What about the lead male dancer? He is the heavy lifter and twirler. Another crisis: He reneges on this responsibility. "I can't do it anymore. They used to be light as a feather. Now they are as heavy as trucks." "UNDERSTUDY, UNDERSTUDY," shouts the impresario from the last orchestra seat. A five foot six, skinny as a rail ballet dancer with form-fitting red tights appears on stage. The director resolves the issue by assigning six members of the chorus to help the understudy twirl and lift. Audience understands. They cheer on each movement. Orchestra makes the most of its most unusual day at the ballet. The box office reports a demand for tickets for an encore performance.

Background Music

You can size up a facility by its background music. The chords reveal management's taste, personality, and successes in operating a business enterprise. Classical music impresses highbrows. They just cannot get enough of Brahms, Chopin, and Beethoven. New arrivals hum familiar passages as they are shown to their tables. The younger set awaits bebop. The music does not disappoint. The jumpy beat quickens the pace. Everyone taps toes and moves around double time. Management understands that the music intended for background has become foreground, requiring a policy change. Sasha, the strolling accordionist, joins the festivities, offering gypsy selections as only Sasha can play them. Finally he concludes with a rousing Cossack song. "It's a cossaska," shouts Kasha Cohen, stirring memories of her home land.

Celebrities and Commercials

Viewers are unaware of the credentials actors need for TV commercials. These actors aspire to appear on stage, screen, and radio. If they fail to connect, they consider TV commercials an important step up their career ladder. Clients look to DOXIE. The actors' studio for TV commercial training. It is interesting to note as DOXIE attaches to realism in seeking actors for a constipation commercial, DOXIE informs candidates that if they do not suffer from that condition, they need not apply. DOXIE lays down equally stringent requirements for Jock Itch. Auditioners must show proof of the malady by bringing along a statement by a board certified dermatologist. Salves that promise dewrinkle are a challenge to DOXIE. Who among their skilled performers are able to play such parts. The files reveal very few. On these occasions, DOXIE draws on their world-wide network of free lancers. An 8 x 10 glossy of Della Course in a prune commercial meets with the CEO's favor. Her face has every line and crevice known to wrinkledom. "Gentlemen, if we can clear up Della Course, we'll all be millionaires." Loud cheers reverberate.

Confused by TV Commercials?

TV commercials confuse and confound. Certain ones make us feel that we made the wrong decision and would be far better off by switching to the company that is the basis of the new ad. Cases in point. Credit cards—own an American Express and feel guilty as hell because Visa is in places where you should be, because not everyone accepts American Express. Long distance phones: If say you have Bell Atlantic, listen to the competition squawk. Serious mistake. Money wasted. Charts and graphs show the error of your ways. Pain persons can take little comfort from watching on TV The Dueling Analgesics. Miracle claims abound for Advil, Tylenol, Ecotrin, to name a few. Who do you believe? Where do you go? You go to seek advice from your friendly pharmacist. Sensing tension, he injects some levity. My advice, take two of these plain aspirins. Call me in the morning. Smiles and Relief.

Double Features

When we were kids, the movie double feature was a way of life, especially on Saturdays—from nine in the morning to what seemed endless. How can we forget seeing the same movies again and again? We turned a double feature into a triple or quadruple. On the screen we saw kid stuff—cowboys, Indians, Buck Rogers, and Flash Gordon. Coming down the aisle, Mother carrying a lunch bag. The noisy throngs did not bother her. The quantity of the bag suggested she was counting on my longer stay at the movies. Midnight was not out of the question based on earlier experiences. Hint of a mass exit was when a break in the film occurred. Many boos and lots of yawns. The End.

Have You Encountered a Scalper?

Scalpers are a special breed of businessmen who make money by procuring tickets for blockbusters and then unloading them to the eager at prices considerably more than the traffic will bear. Where do they operate? Anywhere. Usually you will find them standing in front of buildings within which blockbusters enfold. Theaters, ballparks, concert halls are profitable sites. Scalpers are gabbers. Some even wax poetic, rhyming ticket availability, prices, with names of the featured stars. Brisk business also means SROs and standing ovations. Illegal? Probably. Exorbitant prices? Yes. But hardly a soul resents scalpers. "Leave them alone. It's the only way I can get to see the damn show!" Full support from a satisfied customer.

Identifying a Slacker

Discriminating concert goers at intermissions and after final curtain usually gather to discuss and evaluate. The maestro comes in for his share of praise and blame. Did he draw out the best from the talented group under his baton? High marks but with one exception. Obvious to most were the slacker orchestra players, who just did not contribute. They sat, made playing motions, but let their colleagues do all the work. Slackers. Musicians who do contribute notice the goof offs. Opines a trumpeter, "I blow my brains out, where do these guys get off?" If they won't play, get rid of them. A theme fully endorsed by the strings, wood winds, and kettle drums. The harp demurs on unemployment grounds. The maestro declares that he was engaged to conduct a full orchestra. Slackers beware: "I spend more energy in pumping hands and baton toward the slacker section, begging for a few notes." Stricter rehearsals provide the answer with a full airing of the issue.

Influence of Movies

While growing up we were influenced by many factors. They helped to determine the type of person we would turn out to be. Parents, friends, relatives played an important role. So did teachers. But the most crucial influencer of them all was the movies. Can you deny not wanting to join the posse chasing that dastardly outlaw with Tom Mix and Hopalong Cassidy in hot pursuit? We all suffered the ordeals of those star crossed lovers In *Wuthering Heights*. Admit it. Movies taught us how to behave in social and intimate settings. Remember *Grand Hotel, Gigi,* and *Flying Down to Rio?* We smoked cigarettes like Humphrey Bogart, dangling the reefer on the side of his mouth. Movies taught us how to kiss. When Cary Grant clinched with Ingrid Bergman in *Notorious,* they received standing ovations. So...thank you Joseph Selznick, Daryl Zanuck, Howard Hughes, Cecil B. You made us who we are today!

Is The Radio Really a Lost Art?

In the decade of the thirties, radio was the principal source of family entertainment. At appointed hours and on special days, the clan surrounded that mahogany box from which emitted voices and sounds of the favorite programs of the day. Such satisfaction. Neighbors joined neighbors to form a group of enjoyables. Mood depended on the tuned in personalities. Stalwarts from which one could expect comedy, variety, advice, and high drama included Eddie Cantor of five-daughter fame, Rudy Valley, who generously declared that his time was your time, and Gabriel Heater reporting on wars and kidnappings. Walter Winchell made his presence known from insights of celebrity's private lives to "Mr. and Mrs. America and all the ships at sea." Early day listeners say that TV pales compared with energetic radio. "Those were the good old days."

Late Night Talk Shows

Is it unpatriotic to complain or criticize late night talk shows? Have they become as embedded in Americana as the obligatory playing of the "Star Spangled Banner" at baseball games? Stepping back a few paces, do they deserve such a hallowed place in the national psyche? Two schools prevail (1) Pro—Harmless. Entertaining. Makes you feel good. Sometimes educational. Laughter and chuckles. (2) Con— The host zeroes in on allegedly down-on-the-luck and discredited victims with verve and gusto to the tumultuous approval of the studio audience. Commercials. Guests parade on stage to match wits, but more to plug a movie or a book or as a quid pro quo for the host to return the favor. Commercials. The host vanishes. The band plays a smidgen of an unrecognizable tune. And then a crescendo heralds the host's return. Time runs out with a promise to do it again tomorrow night. I pledge allegiance...

Line Dancers

The moves of line dancers are intricate and demanding. Take, for instance, the grapevine, the vine, a cross over to the left, then back to the right. The shimmy tests rhythm and style. Dancers try but few succeed. But not octogenarian, Sally Suggs. She joins the most robust segments. Shimmy? Sally contorts so feverishly that she could break every bone in her body. The leader senses Sally has inspired, announcing, Six. Seven. Eight. A signal, "LET'S DANCE!" Sally Suggs was never a Radio City Rockette. But in all fairness, she should have been.

Memorabilia

In my barber's shop, entertainment memorabilia line the walls. Tribute to the stars, hung with the skill of a museum curator: photographs, posters, play bills, sculptures, letters provide a viewer with Who's Who, Who Was Who, and What's What. It doesn't take long to recognize the legends. Fred and Ginger. Judy and Mickey. Laurence and Merle. Bette and Joan. Marilyn. Katharine. Akim. Omar. Scan playbills of long runners. "Oklahoma." "My Fair Lady." "Pajama Game." "Guys and Dolls." "Abie's Irish Rose." A treasure trove. But the best is yet to come. A seat in the barber's chair is like front row orchestra. Listen carefully between clips to fascinating show business lore. My barber puts his mouth where his memorabilia is.

Pinch Hitter Concertmaster

The concertmaster first violinist appears on stage to audience applause before the maestro does. Orchestra members fine-tune instruments following the master's decisive tune note, a signal for the waiting in the wings maestro to prepare to enter. Unbeknown to the music world is that a stream of designated pinch players who perform a crucial concertmaster function on call shaking the maestro's hand. They are, in fact, hired for their finger dexterity in shaking. Maestro completes a successful conduct of Mahler's First and detects a pinch player concertmaster. Audience ovation triggers a trip to the pinch player for obligatory handshakes. Maestro shakes with satisfaction. "This pinch player has a great grip. If he could only play the violin!"

Pop Singers

Today's pop singers have strong voices and know how to put songs across. Bruce Springsteen, Billy Joel, Neil Diamond. But I don't relate to them. Call it a generation gap or not keeping abreast of developing sounds that passed me by. I have a mindset for the old singers, and candidly, through memories and 78 and 33 RPMs, they are a pleasure. Remember Kate Smith, the songbird of the south? In my younger days, I joined the nation in hearing her signature, "When the Moon comes over the Mountain." And her stirring, "God Bless America" prompted many to ask for a recall of our beloved you-can't-remember-the-words, "Star Spangled Banner." Personality with a gifted voice, Bing Crosby. His "White Christmas" remains a yuletide classic. Teaming up with Grace Kelly, their duet, "True Love" touches heart stings and moistens eyes. Perhaps the best reason I have remained steadfast to old singers is Judy Garland. "Trolley Car Song." "The Man Who Got Away." And America's all-timer, "Somewhere over the Rainbow." Savor the old singers like rare wine. They improve with age!

Signature Songs

These days when a vocalist continues to popularize a song, it is designated a signature song. It catches on in theaters, concert halls, and on broadcasts. Doobey Doobey Doo. That's Frank Sinatra improvising his signature song, "Strangers in the Night." Taking trolley cars to the stars. That's Tony Bennett in San Francisco where he left his heart in that city by the Bay. "MONA LISA. MONA LISA. MONA LISA." Sung by Nat King Cole, she is a lady like no other. His signature song forever more. "You're lost without a signature song," says an agent to a client. "And I'll help you. Start singing "Swanee River" whenever you can. And that's how Cora Bora made her mark. And with all that, it's time to sign off.

The Wonder of Astaire

Dancers Fred Astaire and Ginger Rogers were America's favorites! Who can forget those movies that they both made—and that stirring music left audiences with a bad case of goose bumps! They came on the scene when the country was in bad shape. A depression loomed. Unemployment was high. Some banks closed. To improve morale, we needed Fred Astaire and Ginger Rogers. They deserve a special place in history! Besides dancing, Fred sang. His voice was delicate but good enough to capture episodes of their movies. In fact, Fred Astaire proved so popular that he appeared on several radio programs. Rudy Valley realized Fred's value and had him as a guest many times. This move resulted in high ratings for the Rudy Valley show!

The Wonderment of Standing In Line

Some say, "Let us pass up that movie. The line's too long." Short sighted. The line can be better than the movie. I have stood in lines hoping they would never end. But I have sat through movies hoping that they would. Your approach and attitude can make your next line experience a winner. After all, a line is a collection of people who are basically strangers. At the outset, you have this common denominator: you all want to see the same movie. That's enough to spark interest and conversation. Of course, your line companions will be those standing in your immediate vicinity, three or four. It amazes how the smiles and exchanges of this small group surge to the last standees. Here are some time-tested subjects to touch off line conversations: Actors (hits, flops, marriages, scandals); family (feuds, broods, prouds, clouds); travel (why, when, where, how.); clothes (style, store, price, practical); food (diets, tryits, swordfish, roughage). It becomes apparent in lines that one or two are frustrated entertainers. They want to sing, dance, or tell jokes. With encouragement, they put forth a wide range of material. Applause motivates. Standees at the end hear and cheer. Ushers signal that it is time to move into the theater. Hugs, embraces, telephone numbers are exchanged. Can the awaiting movie top this?

Ushers

An audience of 200 settles comfortably in their seats in the Kiwanis auditorium awaiting book reviewer, Hortense Hubbell, who will critique *Paul Revere Who Was He, When Was He, Why Was He*. A best seller on the country's reading lists. Organizers confer, causing audience unrest and suspicion. What's happening? Is Hortense Hubbell a no show? Announcement: Hortense Hubbell is a no show. Organizers again confer. What to do? Can't disappoint the comfortably seated 200. Surging down the center aisle, four ushers reach the podium to fill the gap. Usher One grabs the microphone and leads the comfortably seated in a rousing community sing of popular ethnic tunes. Usher Two takes over as a stand-up comic. Audience howls approval at the mirth and good will. The third and fourth usher form a duet, singing nostalgic songs made famous by Jeannette McDonald and Nelson Eddy. An after program comment from a balconyite reflects the sense of all concerned. "Am I glad that Hortense Hubbell didn't show. Those ushers made my day. Bravo!

Encore!

What is an Audience?

Coming from different localities, working at different jobs, blue collar, white collar, professionals, students, housewives, retirees. Separately they show distinct traits. But joined together they form an independent entity, another person who is the sum of their various parts. That union occurs emphatically when strangers become part of an audience. During your next outing at the theater, concert hall, meeting room, or wherever, take stock of yourself and others attending. First clue that you have become an audience is when ushers guide you down the aisle. The more affable introduce you to couples in neighboring seats, grasping at the importance of the occasion. Even before festivities begin, a leader emerges to whom others will follow on when to clap, when to moan, when to snicker, and when to roar. All in unison. Some on-stage performers milk audiences to the extreme with jibes and barbs that are accepted with laughter and goodwill. Prizes and gifts soften the blows. Time expires; the show is over. From audience, you return to individuality. It requires a period of adjustment to just be your old self again.

When is it Right for a Standing Ovation?

I was brought up to reserve a standing ovation for greats and near greats. But in America, the guidelines obscure. My psychologist friend explains. "Some have standing ovation genes. They jump at anything, anytime, anywhere. For research, I attended a play with a patient suffering from S.O. syndrome. Amazing. Her timing was way off. She stood and applauded in the oddest places. Casual dialogue between two minor characters. Scenery changes from bedroom to garden. Notice of cast substitutions. But she is showing slight improvement, no longer applauding cars and furniture." Greats and Near Greats. Does my criteria preclude giving standing ovations to musicians at four-star concerts, performers in smash plays, speakers at forums and seminars? I think so. Those who disagree, "Stand on your own two feet."

Who Holds the Irving Award?

Oscar, Tony, and Irving awards. Annually art committees select the best in the business and present trophies to the deserving at garish extravaganzas. Witnessed by millions on television. Formats are basically the same: Glimpses of the arrivals who immediately become interviewees by breathless reporters; gradual filling up of the cavernous auditorium to the tune of Strike up the Band; introductions of name committee personalities to stir up the crowd with jokes and anecdotes; a somber pause when the accounting firm that tabulated the results is announced. Then on with the show—presenters, awards, envelopes, and speeches shamelessly admitting if it weren't for another "I would not be here tonight." Much applause. Some tears. In the meantime, the Irving award is left unsaid. Its main purpose is to reward the theater goer who has seen the same picture many, many times. It is named after Irving Lutz who holds the record for seeing *The Wizard of Oz* 300 times. "Somewhere over the rainbow…"

Why do we Need Rehearsals?

Rehearsals make or break final performances. For example, dance numbers cannot be taken for granted. Swings. swirls, twirls, and turns have their place on the program. So does a lifting routine by the muscular male lead, holding the prima ballerina high above his head. All these need rehearsals to function smoothly. Without them, swings backfire into glides, twirls into curls, and the prima ballerina loses balance, tumbling into the orchestra pit. Auditoriums and lecture halls are filled with the fidgety, a condition they acquire from listening to unprepared speakers. No rehearsals. Symptoms of the unprepared? (I) Throat clearings before, during, and after. (2) Ahems, Ahs, OH's. (3) Nervous laugh following a not particularly funny passage. (4) Repeating sections covered earlier. (5) Inviting questions, but unable to answer them. The fidgety endure a great deal. They become a captive audience. No way out!

Clothing & Fashion

Packaging Dress Shirts

Men's dress shirts from the factory need undressing to reach the fabric. Handle the process quickly or you may have a handful of tatters rather than a sharply creased ready-to-wear. The first removable is a cellophane covering that should strip off in one piece, but peals off section by section. You are face to face with a shirt. A plastic strip, sharp and firm, encircles the collar with no instruction on how to remove it. A thin scissors to snip nose hair does the job. Next, a price tag is sewing machine riveted to the shirt pocket. In and out, in and out with sharp knife or nose scissors to get rid of the pesky loops. A small folded insert is strung around a button, providing washing and wearing information. It is easy to remove. Finally, pins, pins, pins. The factory folks must have a pin specialist. However, the secret of discovery is a gradual unfolding until you believe this shirt can take its place with others in your wardrobe. Be careful of that one pin around the neck. Get to it before it gets to you.

Slit or no Slits?

"To slit or not to slit, that is the question." Eye the landscape and observe skirts and dresses with no slits, teeny slits at the back of the hem, medium side slits, and the super variety traveling up to the hip and beyond. The conventional approach to "slitting" is to have an undergarment that exactly matches the spacing and does not interfere with the precision intended by the designer. But what if it does? Many women maintain a large inventory of accumulated slips and though they want to be slit stylish are unwilling to part with them. These non-conformists persist in having their way. Beneath the skirts are full-length slips, easily seen through the cracks. Then there are no slips, highly questionable, especially when the skirt or dress has see-through properties. A compromise to avoid feuding and fussing: Put it up to the geniuses of fashion design to develop apparel that appears to have a slit, that looks like it has a slit, but upon close inspection it doesn't. Booming sales, happy customers!

Travel Attire

Little ones are the best dressed at airports. They have it over their adult counterparts, who leave much to be desired. An excellent vantage point to observe comings and goings is to stand at any gate disgorging new arrivals. The mix, you will find, does not discriminate as to sex, age, height, weight, gender, and national origin. But the attire runs the gamut. Obvious are the rear-enders, who sport loose-fitting coverings to minimize bulk. Oscar de la Renta and Ralph Lauren, please note. Here come the baggies: overwhelming amounts of fabric over busy bodies—moving, moving, moving. Colorful sweatshirts with college logos break up the bagginess. Sighting of a female fashion plate stirs interest. From the top of her coiffure to the tip of her Ferragamos, she belongs on the fashion runway. Random men show off their mismatched jackets and pants. A popular sports outfit: Pants that seldom drop down to shoe tops, exposing socks of various hues.

What Happened to Fashion?

A fashion magazine declares, "Women dress to show how they see themselves; they reveal, however coyly, a little bit about themselves. On the other hand, Men dress as they want others to see them. They dress almost always to conceal everything about themselves." What does Wolfgang Wilson think, a freelancer for several Sunday supplements? "Men see a style in a magazine, khaki for instance, and stick to it, sometimes for years." Mike Docket is called the king of denim. He says, "Don't criticize, denim is America's dream! Khaki wearers will give up only when money runs out for those Gap ads. (Truman Capote wore khaki, and so on.)" Felicity Farber in her syndicated column, From Head to Foot, takes issue with women's skirts. "Where is the style? Some are so long they end up beneath ankles; some in the middle drop down to the hamstrings; and some skirts barely cover, risking embarrassing exposures." Wolfgang and Felicity have examined the human condition and found it wanting. What shall it be? Denim. Khaki. Long. Midsize. Short. OR NONE OF THE ABOVE.

Anything Good to Read?

Commentaries

Armrest Wars

Auditorium seat designers provide arm rests for comfort, convenience. When sitting at close quarters, it may turn out that one of the rests may not be exclusively yours. It is the one that divides space between you and your neighbor. Many experience the plop down! Neighbor sighs heavily, then takes over both rests, some pushing aside leaning elbows. Armrest hogs raise the ire of those seated around them. Negotiations among parties do not always work, especially when one is belligerent. Until arm rest guidelines are issued, a fair rule to follow is to allow the ushers to decide by the eenie, minie, mo method. WINNER TAKES ALL!

At The Sound Of The Beep

Phone a "not at homer" and expect to hear a recording that goes something like this. "Esther and Lester are out; At the beep, tell us who you are and why did you call at two in the morning?" Have you noticed when you must leave a message via a recording, your voice loses its naturalness? Psychologist refer to it as the Donald Duck syndrome. "I'll tell you why," explains Florence Lawrence. "It puts me on the spot. I have to talk to no one in particular with feeling and expression. I'm no Sarah Bernhart. There is an alternative, but somewhat risky. Hire a receptionist or two." The danger that lurks is that a receptionist wants to dominate and run things against your better judgment. All considered, the recording wins out!

Audiences Are Crazy

Attending events requiring public mixing is risky business. Danger does not lurk on getting there or on the return trip home. "Beware," warns the magazine, *Audiences Are Crazy*. "Heed persons seated in front, alongside, and to the rear." The centerfold of the August issue features photos so scary with advice to avoid these wackos. "Remain at home and lock the doors." Prominent offenders are painted half faces, usually of the red and blue varieties, super obsessors who bulge over a seat or two and who trudge between rows heading for rest rooms. Animal owners bring pets for a night out. Cats and dogs mingle too freely, making deposits on newly shined shoes. The constrictor brothers, Boa and Noah, show off their namesakes, encouraging petting of their heavy duty reptiles. Those who have difficulty fitting into the scene? *Audiences Are Crazy* says to bring along noisemakers and make your own racket!

Back By Popular Demand

Is the phrase, BACK BY POPULAR DEMAND, a promotional gimmick or are there people shouting, busting down doors, cajoling and pressuring for a reprise of a play, movie, concert, or artist? How can you tell? Ask management and hear the bust-down-doors response with enthusiasm. Poll patrons and the data is mixed. "We enjoyed the show." "Good staging, but much too long." "By popular demand? No one asked me." To settle the issue, I attended several "popular demands" to judge for myself. My first was a movie that I recall had a two-day run at local theaters. If it wasn't liked then, who would like it now? Answer: I and four others who paid the price to see a rerun. My next "by popular" took me to a concert with full-blown orchestra and dueling pianists, playing Gershwin and Mahler. I was surprised when ushers enlisted my help to round up lobby people to fill the hall. The orchestra and soloists, however, demonstrated full-house versatility. Next, an esteemed seminar speaker. Overhead projector, slides, screen, magic markers. He had it all except an audience of ten in a room that seats 100. BACK BY POPULAR DEMAND is after all harmless. Culture and learning may have their place. Whether the phrase stimulates attendance is something else.

Barrels, Oil Cans, or Markers

Are they barrels? Are they oil cans? Are they markers? Each is multi-colored, beginning at the top (orange, white, orange, white, orange), measures about four feet tall; they line walk way, street, road and highway construction sites. Where do they come from? There are so many of them. Possibly oil refineries after contents are emptied. Next census could make an actual count. But the more important issue: can we co-exist with these barrels/oil cans/markers? First, they are far from attractive. You are glad to pass them by, only to notice a new grouping up ahead. Second, they obstruct vision. Those carefully lined up in the A.M. can twist and turn in the P.M. with wind gusts, mischievous kickers, and side swipes. Third, they become collectibles. In the dark of night, antiquarians help themselves to the largess. Since there are so many barrels, etc., their loss is hardly noticed. But can we both co-exist? Can't see why not. They are harmless, make no demands, and are happy to be left alone. Who can ask for anything more!

Can You Pick Out a Kibitzer?

TV networks that broadcast athletic events decide on a format consisting of play-by-play describers plus sports kibitzers who have free reign on what to say and when to grab the microphone, oftentimes interrupting the play-by-play narrative. It is interesting to consider kibitzer credentials. They belong to stars who earned reputations as outstanding practitioners in the sports that they have been hired to kibitz. Listeners detect a tinge of jealousy. Some find it detracting. For example, in the ice skating competition, kibitzer conveys each flaw in the contestant's performance. "I would have done it another way. She's bound to lose points."

Catastrophes

Catastrophes have an afterlife far beyond the actual incidents. Who records these unfortunate events? Historians, writers, and practitioners of arts and entertainment. They are generation informers, conveying in detail the great disasters of our time. Consider TITANIC, a ship laden with luxury, first class passengers, and four gleaming smoke stacks. Iceberg; the Titanic sinks. Its story is maritime lore. Many tell the tale—survivors, crews of sister ships, movie dialog, and lyrics of a rousing Broadway musical. Consider SAN FRANCISCO. The earth shakes, buildings topple, population panics. Clergy conducts services in the streets. Salvation? Positively! The distressed march, single file, into a Radio City-like theater and rejoice. Jeanette MacDonald sings, an omen that all is well. Bravo! It's safe again to leave our hearts with you. So open up your pearly gates.

Cheapos

Tackiest members of society are cheapos, and proud of it. They disdain their accusers as spendthrifts and often wonder how much money these smart alecs have in their savings accounts, referring to their own bank books with confidence. Cheapism takes on various forms, most of which irks others who happen to become involved. Restaurants are a perfect setting to witness the art practiced. Check paying time, dinner for ten. Conventional wisdom—split check to save time. Cheapo has other ideas. Counting on his fingers, to the penny, he announces exactly his share. Moans pass by his deaf ears. The group of ten retires to the lake in the park where wives and lady friends wait near row boats. "Looks as if we will need five boats, two per at five dollars each." Cheapo has other ideas. "One boat will do fine." At dock side, ten gingerly step into a boat built for two. Ashore, sirens scream, guards enter a motor launch. EMERGENCY. Boat with ten, meant for two sinks to the bottom of the lake. Rescued water loggers make their way home to dry out. Cheapo pays the five dollar rental for one boat. A cry goes up, "Banish Cheapo. Let him help someone else save money."

Did They Shorten Your Name?

Scores of immigrants look forward to embarking on our shores for freedom, prosperity, and for shortening their given names—the American way. It doesn't take long for them to acquire their new USA identity. Friends and relatives help. In his native land he was known as Vladimir. "Just call me Vlad," he tells all. In a similar vein, Giuseppe settles on Joe and proud of it. In some quarters, the name Luciano weaves a magic spell. But he understands brevity has its virtue. "I'm Lou and glad of it." We also have in our midst short namers who deliberately make the most of them: CHER, CHARO. TY, SY.

Do You Watch The Movie Credits?

After the movie is over, few of us bother to stick around to see the credits. Who cares? Certainly the people do whose names appear on the screen. Also, their family, friends, studio, and the army of technicians, caterers, and engineers that provide support. Credit reading is revealing and educational. You learn who is behind the movie and how many are involved to put it together. Running down the list, you find titles self-explanatory. Music composer, costumes, art direction, photography, stunts, and more. But not so simple to fathom are terms; Dolly Grip. Key Grip. Best Boy. At first blush, one would think that the Grip family has certain responsibilities. What they are is never told. The mother, Dolly, can well do repair work on clothes heavily used in western scenes. Key, her husband, tends to animals, making sure that none is mistreated. Their son, Best, just looks and listens as a start for a career in the movies.

Doors, Do They Block Our Way?

Above an entrance to a swanky club there is this sign, "Through these doors pass the most important people in the world." Try getting in. Doors block access, not that they are locked or bolted. No, they just confound. To enter the club, pull the outer door; to exit, push. Simple? Not if you are pushing on the outside (instead of pulling) and some well-dressed bon vivant is pulling the same door on the inside (instead of pushing.) Why bother. Break away to the revolving door. Little work. Step into a well-divided compartment, others do the same. And then it's a community round and round, making your way into the building as the door continues around. Avoid rush hour at the revolvers and the frisky crowd. Two or three fill one compartment, usually for fun and games. You step in. Everyone is stuck. Security extricates after a twenty-minute delay. You are again outside looking in. Spying a bar down the street, in the building, you hurry to it. Standing between you and the interior are two swinging doors, wild west style. This time you take no chances and play the waiting game. A customer pushes the doors, you adroitly slip in behind him. Inside, you observe that on the 52nd St. side of the building a wide opening with NO DOORS AT ALL.

Good Old Days

Many times you heard the statement, THOSE WERE THE GOOD OLD DAYS. In fact, you may have mentioned it a time or two. For the record let us analyze it and determine if it has any substance. Case Number One. The speaker recalls his army tour where most of the time he washed dishes. Case Number Two. The speaker tells about his days at Vegas where he lost $500 to the slots, never recovering. Case Number Three. A blind date that cost $175.50. How can those involved say THOSE WERE THE GOOD OLD DAYS? What is your story?

Grab a Seat

The often-used cliché, "Take a load off your feet," invites us to pause, relax, refresh, and SIT. But where and how? That is the question.

Sit-furniture architects close out their designs without ever trying out their creations. Here is a bill of particulars:

Architect A: Your famous style of dining booths doesn't permit a full posterior coverage. Eating on the edge requires patience and balance. Falling out is a distinct possibility.

Architect B: You have pioneered obstructed-vision in theaters, concert halls, and sports arenas. Many wonder how, in the original design, you could have overlooked a clear sighting of the center attraction. Your defense won't wash: "People attend to be seen, not to see." You are the father of discount seats.

Architect C: A more pronounced rising of the floor level could have been eliminated with cushion-carrying. Entertainment-goers resign themselves to looking at the heads of those in front of them. Cushions make viewing more bearable.

To all sit-furniture architects: Sit up and take notice.

Lessons Learned

Why do so many head for aquarium tanks in homes, offices, and dining spots to watch goldfish and their friends swim, splash, and cavort? In some instances, period for observation stretches for days. Tom Scales began the process on World War I, Armistice Day. He still sits with fixed gaze at the fishbowl in cavernous Penn Station, New York. Why? The answer has psychological underpinnings. In 1840 a study of human habits had significant impact on the psychiatric community. "Counsel your patients that fish can solve problems of behavior. Spend time at aquarium tank." Here's what fish watchers can absorb: (1) Appearance. How do fish react to fatigue? LESSONS LEARNED. They work out of it. They are stimulated to their gills. No room in the tank for a sluggish member. (2) Fights and spats. LESSONS LEARNED Fish argue, fight, fuss. Gazers attest to some chasing but, the incident is over in a matter of minutes. (3) Frolicking. LESSONS LEARNED In-the-tank-fun consists of chasing, chasing, chasing. Up and down and all around. In the end no one gets caught! (4) Time for a break, for food and nourishment. LESSONS LEARNED.

Letting Off Steam

The Society for the Egregious meets often. It's a must. Members require this outlet to release steam. Shoddy goods and shoddy treatment are the basis of pent up feelings. Cars are high on the list of the blame quotient. Affected members slice through to the core, describing their woes: lemon, turkey, goofer, guzzler, staler. Member Sol Hocking tells of the treatment he experienced in the service lane of Better Motors. In response to "a loud, grinding noise." "Turn up the radio, you won't hear the noise again." Senior Goldie Golden jumps in slightly out of turn. "Salesman sold me a raised under pillow platform to solve my phlegm problem. Not only did that platform give me more phlegm, I haven't had a good night's sleep in months." Steamer chorus, SUE THE BASTARDS!

Lottery

The lure of big money has grabbed us and won't let go. Lotteries, contests, Publishers Clearing House, to name a few. Take a chance as it's like casino gambling without having to face the slots and croupiers and listening to the machines jangle at jackpot time. Lottery tickets run the gamut. A dollar gives you the chance to scrape off a sliver covering under which reveals prizes won or lost. A bigger ticket has a combination of numbers that can make you rich if you choose the right ones. Here are some common sense tips to ease your journey to prosperity: (1) DO NOT give a friend a lottery ticket as a gift! If you do and she wins a million dollars, you will regret it for the rest of your life. (2) DO NOT seek your pot of gold out-of-town. Play locally. Out-of-town machines favor natives endemic to the regions. (3) And finally, establish a limit on winnings and losings so that you can live again for another day.

Miseries

A person who lives her life on miseries is Greta Trageria. She and others like her are bad-news absorbers. They prick up ears upon hearing about accidents, diseases, sickness, and misfortunes, no matter how serious. They visit devastations to observe first hand. No margin for error for Greta and her gang. Oklahoma City explosion? Jonestown suicides? Floods and hurricanes? Rest assured, Greta and company were there. They are unable to keep their findings to themselves. They gather a wide range of listeners. An opening salvo, "Did you hear about Dobbins..." No matter that the listener doesn't care, never heard of Dobbins, has no interest in Dobbins. What can the medical folks tell us about Greta Trageria? "In childhood her parents told her to stand in a corner and be quiet. Now Greta suffers from the Shush Syndrome."

Other Shoe To Drop

Waiting for the other shoe to drop provides closure—an essential element in life's pursuits. Without it, a continuing pattern emerges, leading to blurs and slurs. Women can shop endlessly UNTIL the loud speakers bark. "SALE. Buy now, no lingering (the shoe)." Matrimony can extend to historic proportions. Then proposal/ marriage (the shoe). Stocks, buy and sell. Fahrenheit for the Rich advises, "Buy at about 45 degrees, Sell at 95, it's too damn hot to hold on to anything." For more shoe-drop data, call 301 LACES. Read SHOE FINDINGS, world-wide shoe drops broken down by continents. Regardless of race, color, or creed. Brace yourself! Next shoe to drop may be yours.

Pairs?

Do good things happen in pairs? We have Huntley and Brinkley, Laurel and Hardy, Astaire and Rogers, and coffee and danish. It must take time to figure out that one. Also some rehearsing! For instance, the commentators have to review facts before presenting them. Astaire and Rogers danced together many times before their finales on the screen. If true, find yourself a partner and make the most of it.

The Sound of Silence

In hospitals, libraries, and other places a prohibitive word looms large, near and far: SILENCE. The message is clear. No talking, no gabbing, no fooling around. The younger set kicks up the most dust. They cavort under large SILENCE posters, a flagrant violation. The older set steadfastly observes the policy, but you can see they are bursting to say something if they only were granted freedom of expression. Consider. Is the SILENCE policy invoked in the right places? Take libraries as an example. You read, study, memorize, fill your head with facts and figures, just to keep things bottled up. SILENCE or commit a breach of the code. Hospitals ask that you please check any noise and chatter at the door. SHUSH. Keep to yourself that your kin improves, that the doctor encourages, that the hospital says "take him home." SHUSH. Not really. Set aside areas that will accommodate various emotions. SCHMOOZ ROOM. CHATTER BOX. WHISPER ALCOVE. TOT SPOTS. COMIC CUBICLES. Oh yes, SILENCE and SHUSH.

Titles

Our society provides an easy way to respect and admire. Titles. Listen to someone's name—say Sharon Dickens, and in and out it goes, joining the other names you hear during the course of the day. But listen or read, Honorable Sharon Dickens, you pause and take notice. The Honorable is right up there. She can sit on the bench as a judge bedecked in black judicial robes and gavel in hand to maintain proper decorum. Honorable entitles Sharon Dickens to a place in a legislative body—Senate, House, Assembly. Honorable also precedes the names of Governors and Mayors. Some disregard proper usage and attach Honorable to their name as an image builder. They go all the way, insisting on Esquire to make sure. Thus: Honorable Fred Fliegel, Esquire. (Fred works in maintenance at the Zippo Mall.)

Unforgettable

It shouldn't be that way, but some unforgettable persons are forgotten—too soon. Take Betsy Ross as a for instance. Her picture adorns history books, sewing our American flag. She is the nation's first seamstress. So much more can be done to pay her homage. Would it violate some master plan to make Flag Day, Betsy Ross Day? Why not hang out the Stars and Stripes in Betsy's honor? Then the Moses family deserve their due, Grandma and her son, Biblical. How we admire their lives and teachings. The parting of the waters suggests a swim fest or a Moses Marathon. World famous athletes will unite in brotherhood and sisterhood. Ludwig Von Beethoven fades away. This great composer barely hangs on in memory through the first stirring notes of his Fifth Symphony "DA DA DA DA." But more than that is required to commemorate his genius, to repay the riches that he has bestowed on us. At an appointed hour, perhaps after sundown, every symphony orchestra convenes to play every Beethoven symphony to their local audiences. A crescendo of Beethoven's music cascades around the world.

What Are The Mysteries of Towels?

Towels in strange surroundings confuse. At a friend's house, you need to dry yourself after a wet encounter. On a special rack, there are plenty to choose. Recollection! Those are company towels.

Host establishes this category, implying, "Hands off the good stuff." It appears rack towels consist of remnants. "So what?" remarks a potential user. "Don't be so picky." It is, however, unusual to discover these terms emblazoned on a towel you select: Mr. and Mrs. His and Hers. Itsy and Bitsy. Sexy. Charmer. Boobie. Turn Me On. Diet Coke. Anacin. 911. Most times, the BYOT principle applies: That is, Bring Your Own Towel. As a goodwill gesture, take along an extra for the company rack, emblazoning a message of your own: *RETURN TO LENDER.*

What Are Your Odds?

At casinos, racetracks, lotteries, and emporiums, odds are king. If they favor you, expect to hear such terms as (1) jackpot. (2) daily double, (3) power ball, (4) bonus and dividends. At these venues, advice is plentiful, but for a set fee. Canny Gershwind, a legend on the gambling scene, specializes in race tracks. His admonition has saved clients a fortune: "Horses are trained to win, place, or show exactly according to how the track wants them to," His book, *Horses Make Sense* has been a best seller for eighty-nine weeks... Pierpont Moran, Wall Street mogul, couldn't be more explicit. "Play the slots, lose your shirt. Odds favor the house." An occasional winner disagrees, counting fifteen dollars in change. Pierpont smiles as he observes the "winner" plough the gains back into the slot machine. Want a sure thing? Save stamps.

What Happened to the Word Manners?

What has happened to word manners and what it stands for? Yesteryear, it meant so much and was the topic of Conversations. Warning to whomever violated existing standards, his behavior was on the lips of the manners keepers as an example of what to avoid. Experts who study these matters declare that good manners should be practiced at the dinner table and in social situations. Question? Who keeps track of whom?

Who is in
Cartoon Heaven?

In cartoon heaven, stalwarts regale, celebrating years of service in comic strips that bear their names. Virtually gone, but far from forgotten—MOON MULLINS, WINNIE WINKLE, DICK TRACY, MAGGIE AND JIGGS, ANDY GUMP, LITTLE ORPHAN ANNIE, and a score of others. In a sense, they have been rewarded. At their peak and in cartoon heaven, never will they age or grow old. We will remember them as they are, as they were. And as they always will be.

Why Are We Superstitious?

We Homo sapiens are a superstitious lot. In calmer days, we take full credit for the pluses. In darker days, we point fingers and place the blame. It's strange that athletes experience a kind of voodooism. To them Sports Illustrated covers are poison. When issues hit the newsstands, their team hits the skids. Joel Purchase avoids black cats and overhead ladders. He collects bubblegum baseball cards. "Want to be close to heroes I admire," says Purchase. Wonder of Wonder. Joe DiMaggio happens to walk into Joel Purchase's civics class. He walks right up to Joel and thanks him "for collecting my portrait." Warm handshakes and a tender of free passes to Yankee Stadium. Superstitious no more, Joel Purchase disposes of the twenty-nine rabbit feet he was carrying in reserve.

Woes of Construction

Bring on the cranes. Make way for the trucks. Here come the bricks, cement, and mortar. Laborers, hard hats in place, converge. A perfect start for a construction site. Little doubt what construction people do. They carve out cities, towns, villages, and hamlets. They mold the landscape, create skylines, build houses and bridges, scoop out rocks and earth from mountains for tunnels, streets, and roads. "Progress at a price," say the impatients. Construction snarls traffic, blocks access, confuses pedestrians, makes loud noises, slops up neighborhoods. "There has to be a better way." Are we to become a generation of double parkers, grid lockers, stumbling to the Saint Tinnitus Dance? Ponder this. Will construction destroy our American way of life? I PLEDGE ALLEGIANCE.

Commerce & Money

Buy & Return

Have you ever thought about who shops at department stores and why? I was never mindful until one day it became necessary to return two turtle neck sweaters, Flaw—excessive spaciousness; price—$19.40 for both. Directed to Customer Service on the fourth floor, I estimated how long a wait, for at least thirty were lined up in front of me. Of course, it would depend on the nature of each problem and the efficiency of the server to solve it. A veteran of Customer Service lines broke the tension by volunteering his assessment, "You can expect an hour delay." Almost accurate, it took two hours. The question: "Do customers buy or do they return?" Shoppers have a you-can-always-give-it-back mentality encouraged by salespersons, friends, and curious onlookers. A rack observer specializing in merchandise flow says, "You can see the stuff leaving the racks and coming right back. Leaving and coming back. Forget about those sales and ads. The shopper has returns in mind before entering the store!"

Do You Buy Retail?

Woody Allen told the story, I believe, that a friend (perhaps himself) was looked upon with disdain because he bought retail. Unquestionably, discount is America's theme. Most revealing when you proudly boast of a gold-plated purchase and hear that you could have done better at Zupps at a 25 percent discount. Newspaper ads, special mailings, TV commercials keep up the discount drumbeat, mostly brand names and yours for the buying. There is no shortage of places when you decide on discount. Even department stores, recognizing the fever, scream discounts in their regular shopping ads in local papers. Buyers closely attuned to prices and products eventually find their way to outlet stores. They spring up in the malls, suburbs, and roadsides, and from all appearances are here to stay. Outlets are diversified or specialized, but all at discounts. Parking lot license plates indicate thoroughly traveled clientele. Before leaving on a trip to Madrid, a tourist learned only one Spanish word: DESCUENTO (DISCOUNT).

Does the Shoe Fit?

Survey the buying public as to who shows understanding and patience under fire, you will find shoe salesmen high on the list, even perhaps number one. Shoe salesmen? Many would question this heavy favorable vote. But judge for yourself. Business is brisk at Shoester's Originals. Salesmen running to and fro and customers vying for attention. At Shoester's, as at most stores, customers are up front and boxes shelved in the back. Understanding and patience. The Sonya and Sam Show—customer Sonya is greeted by salesman Sam with a sincere, "What can I do to help you?" "Yes," says Sonya, "I need a 9 wide, very wide because of my bunions." Back to the shelves dashes Sam, returning with five boxes of different styles and colors, straps, laces, and open toes. Remembering the bunions, Sam carefully shoe horns the first pair. No! The second pair. No! The third pair. No! On and on to the fifth pair, No! A disappointed Sonya, but an undaunted Sam. Leaving the five boxes for later collection, Sam drains the back shelves of twelve more boxes, included among them are ballerina slippers and clodhoppers. Sonya and Sam get along famously all during the try-ons. Entering is Sonya's Significant Other, not as patient as Sam. He signals. Sonya obeys and walks away. Sam calls out that he'd like to show her a line just received. Good-bye waves. No sale. No commission. Seventeen boxes to restore and put back. A smiling Sam seems up to the task as he eyes another customer. "Without bunions, I hope."

How Do We Know The Correct Price?

Back Saver; Treat your back to the world's stress-free recliner." So says the ad. It holds out the promise for you to abandon Backache Sufferers of America, to which you have belonged since bending down to pick up a banana peel. Of course, you are willing. But how much does the recliner cost? Guess. No price in the ad. "They've got a secret." Call or write to find what it is. This next ad attracts, offering a little of Austria and a lot of Vermont. It's all yours, 2000 rolling acres amid spectacular mountain views at the Trapp Family Lodge. How much does this one cost? Guess. The ad does not provide a clue on what it would take to spend a week with the Trapps. Close the magazine, switch on television. In living color, you witness a vast array of cars that "will be in your dealer's showroom this Friday." The cost. Guess. On screen, you see tantalizing statements to influence your decision-making. "Shockingly Affordable." "No Haggling." "Take Your Time To Pay." "Tires Checked for the Life of the Car." Marketing Expert, Vera Flatbed, who has written on the subject of hidden pricing, has this astute observation. "Candidly, prices are so high that vendors fear revealing the exact numbers to consumers." We, therefore, now live in a world of the internet, catalogs, and 800 numbers, a trend that I'm afraid will continue in the foreseeable future.

Inspectors

"I have personally examined every detail of this garment to make sure it meets our high quality standards. Thank you for buying our product." 35. Inspectors by number. So many of us would like to know who is 35. Robert Bixby, age 43, has five kids, active PTA member, church goer, ardent stamp collector. Rapid advancement on the job. Once was Number 11. Similarly, his colleagues deserve to have the veil lifted as well. And 14, 9, 23, 41, 62, and 55 languish in anonymity, composing statements on the worth of the product. In a far off dark corner sit 2 1/2, 7 3/4, 18 7/8. They have been "fractionized" for some disagreement or run-in with the shop foreman.

Money Back Guarantee

Money back guarantee, you hear about it, read about it, and want to take advantage of it. The sense of the phrase offers to return what you paid for a specific item, particularly if you are not satisfied. Let's test that thesis. Sam Bygone drives a new sedan to the show room, complaining that the motor makes strange noises. He wants his money back! "Try and get it! "You kept the car too long beyond the money back period. The best we can do is to fix the motor at a cost of $75. If the motor acts up again, turn on the radio so you won't hear it."

Need a CPA?

Myron has never received a CPA diploma but he displays CPA tendencies. Show him some figures and in a flash he constructs a Profit and Loss Statement and a Balance Sheet, all from the mind. His work tools are a number 2 pencil and a yellow legal size pad. No calculators and computers for Myron. "I just don't trust them." He assists special clientele, especially during tax time. They line up in front of his apartment, waiting turns. An H & R Block outlet down the hall takes notice. With unlimited skills, why is Myron just a bookkeeper in an obscure firm on skid row? Debit, Credit. Debit, Credit. Make room for the Myrons of this world! In government, they can show ways to reduce deficits and lower taxes; in business, they can explain what GNP, GDP, and COLA mean; in art and entertainment, they can advise a sensible and affordable pricing policy at the box office. We have geniuses in our midst. Offer them a special place without diplomas.

Selling Through Classifieds Ads

It takes a knack to sell household goods through the classifieds. You have to inject verve in ads to make potential buyers take notice. Forget marginal prose. You won't have any nibbles. Also, repeat ads run up the bill. Sample: You decide that your trusty skis have served you well on the slopes. But they have enough slide in them to serve another. An ad, "Skis for sale, willing to sacrifice," will not go anyplace. But, "Buy my skis, recently used on the Swiss Alps" has possibilities. Sample: Selling items barely in working order is a challenge. "Visit us for bargains," is foredoomed. But "A tinkerer's 'and mechanic's' paradise," will attract hordes. Sample: How do you lure a potential to want a TV aerial located high on your roof. Poor Listing—"TV aerial in good condition." Better Listing—"Junk your rabbit ears. Climb our roof and take away aerial for picture perfect reception."

Telemarketers

Telemarketers call at meal time, the best chance they can establish contact. In answering, the respondents become irritated. And for good cause. "Why," they ask, "must I answer questions between spoonfuls of shish kebab and dessert?" Then come the speeches. Telemarketers must convey the biggest picture that sometimes includes eligibility for vacation travel and frequent flier points. Catalog purchases are also on the agenda. They promise to send a complete list of merchandise available for bargain purchases. They assure follow-up calls to learn of your decision. Expect to hear from them during meal time.

The Barn Policy

An advertising ploy that is growing popular involves the barn merchandising method. Consumers respond. They feel sellers are reaching out to attract a diversity of worthwhile goods and services. Listen to an enthused potential, "When I see the word barn, you can bet I'll be there." And he is. He shops at the Food Barn. Shoe Barn. Furniture Barn. Auto Barn. Mattress Barn, Rug Barn. Fruit Barn. Coffee Barn. Viagra Barn. Here's the deal. Pick out the product that you like. Then take it away at substantial savings. No arguments. Prompt refunds. That's barn policy.

What Happens in Financial Markets?

Investors in financial markets have to follow the ups, the downs, and the stand stills. Media reports the data on radio, TV, and in the comprehensive listings in the daily newspapers. Lingo bandied about on the trading floors and in local brokerage houses confound non investors: BULL, BEAR, NASDAQ, DOW JONES. Erratic behavior of key indicators cause some to withdraw from the fray. What does Dow Jones say? "Sit tight." Obviously when the market yo-yos it creates a panic situation, causing investors to research what happened during previous plummets. They have no basis for optimism. Market crashes. Traders floating out windows. Blue chips going bankrupt. Freelancer, Stack Split, eases the pain. He hovers over the worst case scenarios with strategies to beat the falling dominoes. He puts a positive spin on a situation that looked hopeless. When trading, you don't have to look for Stack Split. He will find you!

Why 99 Cents?

What's with this 99-cent pricing policy? Ads are full of it. Do merchants think consumers lack the arithmetic skills and don't know what's going on? Examples: Haggar Wrinkle-Frees, $31.99; Sterling Chokers, $19.99; Oil Drainers, $8.99; Straw Handbags, $39.99; Men's Designer Sports Coats, $169.99; Pound of Lox, $22.99; Vanity Fair Bra—all cup sizes, $16.99; and so on. The true price reveals itself at the cash register. Ninety-nine centers of this world, wise up! Consumers want to know the exact cost. Send the 99ers to numbers heaven for much-needed R&R.

Wrapping And Packing

Wrapping and packaging are the final touches of a store purchase. The state of the art has advanced so far that the decorated boxes look better than their contents. Old-timers marvel at the results, some recalling primitive packaging days when fish were wrapped in newspapers. "I remember reading blurred headlines on the body of the fish." In contrast—buy a sweater, a tie, gloves, perfume, hand lotion, and expect a cornucopia of packaging. Your choice depends on whom you want as your wrapper of record. Salesperson will offer to package your purchase. Accept and you have a neat bag or box. Awaiting, if you care to use them, are the wrapping and packaging specialists. They are so good that they free lance at Embassy functions. At packaging school they learn "Make your work so outstanding that the recipient will decline to open the package for fear of cutting the ribbon and upsetting your design." Finally, salespersons recognize do-it-yourselfers. They are legion of the shopping community. They are given wrappings and ribbons and leave the store looking forward to an exciting experience. And that's a wrap.

Communication –
Reading, Writing,
Listening, Speaking

Anything Good to Read?

Reading in the bathroom is a national pastime. Days of bashfulness and cover-up are long gone. In fact, many proudly announce their destination and ask advice on the type of reading material to take with them. As volumes accumulate, bathroom libraries emerge to accommodate varieties of newspapers, magazines, technical reports, books, medical articles, photos, and personal correspondence. Most popular bathroom fare is comics, sports, and People Magazine. Books have an attraction for long-term users and those who are required to make frequent return trips. Literature is replete with stories resulting in educational benefits from bathroom reading. The annals glowingly report a recent Ph.D. recipient boned up for his degree behind closed doors. A role model.

Are You a Scanner?

Why is it that when opening a book or magazine, the first place readers go is to pictures, cartoons, and comics. They overlook the text although it tells the story which is why the author wrote the piece in the first place.

It is the basis for commentary, and it takes the most time to write. Why? Readers look for short cuts. They are overwhelmed by volume. They pause, skip over pages, and decide to focus on photos and drawings.

The more daunting then declare they read the entire work, offering a review and synopsis. Authors can do a great deal to help these unfortunates by organizing their material to recognize reading patterns.

Customer Comment Cards

You find them in the mail. You see them slipped under the hotel room door. You spot them with new appliances, TVs, VCRs. They are customer comment cards. Recipients pay no mind to them; initiators pray for their return. Example: We study your comments, follow up on them, and direct our staff to respond to your needs… We take your evaluation seriously. And we're committed to your total satisfaction. How do you balance the throw-it-away mentality with help-us pleadings? To start with, you avoid turn off questions: (1) Did the staff display nothing's-too-tough-for-us attitude? (2) Name items found in your room that shouldn't have been there. (3) Did the dining room satisfy your palate? How and why? (4) Would you recommend us to a friend? All no replies will be pooled for a drawing. The prize: An all expense stay at this hotel for one week. Good Luck!

Do Writers Put Words In Your Mouth?

Did you realize writers of plays, TV, and movies put words into your mouth? You become addicted. You marvel at the crispness and pungency of their dialog. Vocabulary show-stoppers that you use in speeches, conversations, and articles. From Broadway comes the irregular cadence count—six, seven, eight. A favorite of chorusmeisters and dance teachers. One, two, three has suffered the fate of the dinosaurs. Interviewers say, "Let's take it from the top." Many find from the top handy, although some confess they feel confused as to the precise meaning. Perhaps Rhett Butler's reply to Scarlett's rejection will be forever on our lips. FRANKLY, MY DEAR, I DON'T GIVE A DAMN!

Is English Troublesome?

So many find English so troublesome. They skewer sentences from unrecognizable into complete oblivion. Why does this mangling occur? (1) Visitors to our shores arrive with few language credentials. They superimpose their mother tongue over most English words, phrases. Push becomes shtoop. Carry, shlep. Wow, OO LA LA. (2) Absorbers have little idea about English, particularly its structure and its purpose. They listen to the worse speakers and read literary dribble, applying them as models in conversation and correspondence. (3) Ethnics preserve their roots—and proud of it. Nasalities, gutturals, and twangs tell about the speaker's origin but hardly clarify the message. (4) A National Bad English Convention provides resources to the troubled as well as uplifting spirits. Useful features: awards for Congeniality. Englishism. Most Likely to Succeed. The convention includes a rousing song performed by venerable Bert Parks, "I can do it, so can you!" Standup comic, Val Seltzer, adds levity with his broken English jokes. Exit polls indicate a smash hit. Siskel and Ebert give it a rare ten fingers up.

Listen Up

Who listens? Few, if any. Test yourself. Deep in conversation with a friend, he provides a twenty minute discourse on the equator. Do you care? Do you have a mind fadeout? Do you listen? We retain only 20 percent of what we hear. And there is also a strong tendency to prepare your answer while you are hearing all that equator talk. However, we should not dismiss what others say to us. Intermingled among useless rhetoric, there could be some morsels of wisdom, surprising revelations that can be used to good advantage. It takes training and discipline to listen. Eye gaze is important. (l) As the receiver, you must keep eyes firmly fixed on the sender as the message makes its way to your ears. It is difficult, but you must forsake eye and head movements in mid conversation. (2) For training, tune in on the most boring television program to its conclusion. This will create discipline needed to manage various listening situations. (3) Finally, a barrage of strategic questions aimed at the sender creates special effects that make the conversation go every which way. It has been documented that this approach can take hours until the time is consumed between sender and receiver and no one remembers what was first said.

Listening To The Radio

Drive out of town and you soon turn on the car radio to break the monotony. Have you tuned in programs lately, much less worked the dials and buttons (skim, scan, tune)? The stations fade as you drive away from their antennas. Consider that a relief from the programs some offer. Let us ride on the open road and listen together. Judge for yourself. We shove off from home and the listening is easy. Local stuff. Pat In the helicopter reporting traffic snarls on the Beltway; Boris Hillman forecasting a stock surge (market plummets 62 points); Buddy playing Glen Miller, Tommy Dorsey, and Horace Heidt; Nina Consuega interpreting on the Spanish language station; and Maynard holding down the charts on the 24-hour weather station. As we move away, the radio becomes testy. Static, some gurgles. New stations are poised to take over. Never mind their call letters; they blast their calling cards in the form rock and roll singers and bands, past and present, panels of experts on sundry subjects, talk show jockeys fielding questions, and at the remotest end of the dial, Beethoven's "Pastoral" on the good music station. Fade out. New venue, other shows. Doubled up stations are source of irritation. None makes sense. The road narrows, rock and punk dominate. As for Beethoven, he's long gone. My riding companion advises, "Turn it off, turn it back." Makes sense. We return to the soothing voice of Pat in helicopter gasping about the tangle on the Beltway. That's nothing Pat, compared to what we have been through on the radio.

Numbers Game

In the telephone arena, hi-tech can drive you crazy. Commit to a system and endless options prevail. One option protects against missing calls when you are absent or when you just don't care to answer. A button push restores the voice of the original caller. The busies in our society have opted for the numbers plan. It works like this: You are online with a stockbroker. You hear, "If you want quotations, press one." "If you want Dow Jones, press two." "If you want a broker, sorry none is available, press three." "If you wish to talk anyone, press six" "Thank you for your patience." Problem when playing the numbers game. The folks aren't around when their number is up. Redial and expect a rerun of numbers: Low tech.

Overcoming Stage Fright

Stage fright is the bane of communication both in public and private. It afflicts the most experienced from those who speak to large audiences to persons who are asked to just say a few words at a meeting. Symptoms gripping the frightened include panic, terror, numbness, sweaty palms, and the shakes. Advice for relieving pain is abundant. It varies from forceful to gradual. The forceful approach spells out to hang in there. Smile. Put on a happy face. "I'd rather heal in small doses." A viewpoint. That is when the gradual approach comes in. Candidates are taught to sectionalize; that is, deliver messages in bits and pieces. Split up paragraphs, sentences if it provides a comfort zone. Specialist, Louis Posture, advocates forceful, while Dora Vowels, the gradual. She says, "Why frighten the daylights out of them. We will have a generation of stutterers. Piece meal. Slow and steady." A paralyzed of audiences victim retorts, "Nothing works. For me three martinis do the job.

Speech somewhat slurred, but am I relaxed!" Posture and Vowels add it as a stage fright remedy. Remember, when facing an audience, think about the less fortunate and the available options to see you through: (1) forceful, (2) gradual, (3) three martinis. Take your pick.

Proper Words

Linguist Sheila Shackelford stunned a lunch audience with her keynote speech remarks about shrinking word stock. "We have to admit that when Americans reach out for the proper word, they find the door shut. What do they do? Insert sound-alikes that are far from the target." Sheila tried to prove her thesis with the word CONDIMENT. "Who knows that meaning?" Sheepish expressions around the room. Biff, in quick response, points to the mustard jar on his table. Sheila Shackelford: "Here are the alternatives used for CONDIMENT, food seasoning. CONDOM (protective device for sexual encounters), CONDOR (huge vulture), CONDOMINIUM (trendy priced apartment that owner buys and refers to as 'my house.' Any questions?" "Ms. Shackelford. Who gives a damn?" A unison reply from most, "We give a damn. Thank you, Sheila!" Do you?

Send the Anchor

Are they God? Some think so. The network news anchors enjoy a special place in the U.S. bosom. Imagine a late breaking news event without seeing an anchor's face. In fact, they all can converge at one time in one place searching for a hot scoop. Strife in Bosnia, send the anchor; mid-west floods, send the anchor; California mud slides, the anchor; presidential travel and vacations, the anchor. It is interesting to note that networks have outstanding, skilled personnel who can handle these assignments, many of whom live or work in the targeted locality. No, send the anchor. The meaning of this seems clear: the public needs anchor reassurance that all is well. Not to worry.

The Sound of Your Voice

Sy Tryon likes to sing to break monotony and to hear his own voice capture the tunes that he found unforgettable in bygone days. He displays zest, mouthing words and phrases with great expression and adding orchestral accompaniments such as, "Da da da da, Oo oo oo oo, Sh sh sh, La de da." His audience? Anyone who will listen. To some this creates a problem, especially those who want peace and who think that Sy is a lousy singer. How would you rate Sy Tryon? Fun and uplifting? Public nuisance? Opinions vary in a recently conducted survey. "Leave him alone. Let him sing all he wants. This troubled world can use more Sy Tryons." Opposing, a zealot emphatically registers this negative. "Lock him up and throw away the key. We don't need to hear his arias. Let him practice in the shower."

What Do Different Words Mean?

George Bernard Shaw has been said to remark that the main element that separates the British from Americans is the English language. Curious. Have we Americans, in our fight for independence, violated the mother tongue that much? In London or Yorkshire, to reach the top floor of an office building you take a LIFT. In New York or Philadelphia, an ELEVATOR. Same conveyance, different names. Quaint row houses in Kensington are advertised or leased as FLATS. In the U.S. urban areas, APARTMENTS. Driving on British roads, you soon meet ROUNDABOUTS, on which cars turn slowly and at angular patterns until they reach the straight flat road ahead. On U.S. roads and traffic hubs, you yield and blend into CIRCLES. UNDERGROUND is the name of London's speedy transit system. In the states, it is METRO; BART, IRT, BMT are SUBWAYS by any other name. In British parlance, GAOL stands for JAIL or KLINK. BOOT is TRUNK; a HOOD is a BONNET; SEXY is DISHY. George Bernard Shaw may have had it right about the language separation.

What Happened To Handwriting?

A good handwriting doesn't run in the family. One sister displays a flowing script that Thomas Jefferson would have welcomed on the Declaration of Independence team. Her four siblings cause much head scratching. "What in the world is that all about?" We are handwriting weaklings. Educators recognize the deficiency. In many schools, they encourage switching bad writers to printers, that is printing words in upper and lowercase. They also recommend intensive handwriting refreshers, even if it means starting from scratch. Where did we go wrong? When did a pleasant and acceptable handwriting find itself at the back of the bus? We left the starting gate in good shape. After graduating kindergarten, penmanship began to dominate the curriculum in our tender years. On lined pads we penned adjoining concentric circles and up and down lines, a prelude to writing words and phrases. Teacher's goal was for us to enter the outside world, polished and accomplished. Fate interceded. In academia, penmanship became a casualty. In an office setting, you scribbled to complete the assignment. "I need the report yesterday," so said the boss. Good intentions, bad results. A secretary confessed at a seminar that her boss wrote so poorly that he brought his papers to her and asked, "What did I say?" If it gets that bad, have someone else do it for you. No shame.

What is an Acronym?

Acronym is a word formed by extracting the first letters from a name. Recall those smartly dressed patriotic WAVES? That was the acronym for Women Accepted for Volunteer Emergency Service.

Need advice and a loan to establish a business of modest proportions? Call SBA, acronym for the Small Business Administration. Before listing a few guidelines, it should be made clear that acronyms are not abbreviations, although that's what they are considered in some circles. They sound like abbreviations, they look like abbreviations, they are confused with abbreviations. But they are not. The guidelines: First, write out a complete name: International House of Pancakes. Second, next to it, in parentheses, write the acronym (IHOP). You are home free! Shed parentheses and use acronym all the way. IHOP, IHOP, IHOP. Now comes the delicate part. How to handle, say, Association of Social Scientists (ASS), Baltimore Opera Professional Singers (BOPS), Champion Riders Uniformed Desperadoes (CRUD)? Under these circumstances, take no chances—WRITE OUT COMPLETE NAME WHENEVER IT APPEARS.

What is the Mystique of Crossword Puzzles?

Crossword puzzle fans steer clear of Sonny Dale. He became intrigued to fill in the squares. It all began with an over-the-shoulder glance. Seated next to a puzzle aficionado on the L2 bus, Sonny just couldn't help working on the other guy's puzzle mentally. Wouldn't you expect it? Enthusiasm has no bounds. Sonny Dale, pencil in hand, feverishly makes entries while the other guy looks in astonishment. A slight problem does ensue, and that is why fans steer clear. All Sonny's entries are wrong and border on the absurd. Seminars deal with the Sonny Dales of this world. Unconventional, they make up words and phrases and squeeze them into the allotted space. They are not role models. In fact they give crossword puzzling a bad name.

What is the Wonder of Jokes?

Jokes are brighteners. They jump-start a lagging conversation. They pepper reunions. They uncover a life of that not everyone can deliver. You probably have suffered the ordeal of listening to Hy unload his material; many laugh but he isn't funny. Hy never knows when to conclude, probably because with each joke he goes into convulsions, no one else does. Doug has a reputation for silence. He listens, smiles, and observes an economy of expression. A Doug witticism comes out when least expected. Audience howls. If you are inclined to use brighteners, consider the following ice breakers: (1) A Midwesterner struggles in the desert crying for water. Struggler is offered 100 ties for $50. "Water, water." "Fifty ties for $10." "Water, water." "Down the hill, knock on the door." Struggler knocks on the door, "Water, water." Response: "Sorry you cannot get in without a tie." (2) A customer limps up to the pharmacist, asking for a can of talcum powder. "Walk this way," is the helpful reply. Customer: "If I could walk this way I wouldn't need the talcum powder." (3) A bus accident immobilizes Mr. Ginsberg. As he lies on the pavement, a sympathetic onlooker approaches and tucks a pillow beneath Ginsberg's head. "Are you comfortable?" "Yes, thank you."

Why a Lull in Conversation?

At parties, meetings, and receptions, a glaring problem moves up front and center: lulls and gaps in conversation. Listen in. You seldom hear a smooth flow of words. People seem to have difficulty talking to each other. Instead of a constant stream of conversation that interests, you hear small talk, jabberwocky, babble, and those lulls and gaps. Aha, ahem, rule the day with some stale jokes interspersed. Hosts and hostesses put great stock in making sure they invite the right people who can sustain a conversation. Without them, their functions deteriorate into ahas, ahems, and throat clearings. If you have a gift of gab and a point of view, your check may be in the mail.

Why Ghost Writers?

At the summit of world leaders, homage was paid to their ghost writers. About time. Writers for these summiteers put words in their mouths, ideas in their heads that go down in history. Thaddeus, it is written, was one of first ghostwriters. His Client: Moses. Both argued about the phraseology of the Ten Commandments. "Whoa MO," said Thad, "Your writing has to be good. It's cast in stone and for the ages. Who is going to use the Thou lingo years from now? Tell you what, take this drill, and carve your words into these two tablets, walk down the mountain, and show them to that crowd below, and let's see what happens." Joy. Rejoicing. Freedom. Thad, up above, shrugged, "It will never catch on. All those Thou's will interfere with the message.

Why Junk Mail?

Mailboxes throughout the land are stuffed with a variety of items that puzzles recipients. Junk mail some call it. They review the assortment as they ask why? who? where? and how? You would too if the superfluous included outdated magazines, hats, gloves rope, toys, and photos of persons you've never met. Here's what you do to curb the outrage. In the short run (1) cancel magazines including first edition, How to Look Ritzy and Glitzy. (2) Destroy the six new credit cards, writing a note of abomination to the sender. (3) Donate all garments and toys to Goodwill. Here's what you do in the long run. (a) Dump remaining goods in a garbage bin. (b) Disregard annoying follow-up communications. (c) Refuse awards such as free trips to Vegas and Tahoe. If you follow these guidelines, next time you open your mailbox, you can shout, "Free at last, Free at Last, thank goodness, I'm Free at last."Ejp

Who Pays the Check?

Dining & Food

All Aboard

Cruises attract certain types who make their presence painfully obvious aboard ship. The hearty appetizers dominate much of the scuttlebutt. Shipmates know when the hearties sign up, they seldom ask about ports of call but for the menus and composition of the midnight buffet. Cruise lines try to satisfy these voracious eaters, unfurling strategies often used in gourmet restaurants.

(1) Their cabins are located adjacent to a designated dining room, just seconds away from ground zero. (2) Sanctions are imposed on tablemates who gab during meal servings. (3) Appetizers are given access to all dining rooms, usually numbering six. They can and do partake in several daily breakfasts, lunches, and dinners. Hunger pangs? Easy to satisfy with frequent on-deck refreshments from stem to stern. Jollies are cruise regulars. For them, ships are ideal to try out stale jokes that no one bothers listening to on land. They masquerade, sing, jig, and form groups to meet at reunions. Smiling as they ascend the gangplank are the discounters, poised to present tickets to the collector, who punches them below the 50 percent line. Discounters enrage others, who paid full fare, boasting of their coup. Complaints reach the bridge where the captain has steering responsibilities. He immediately orders an across-the-board 10 percent ticket reduction for all passengers, preventing a rumored mutiny.

All You Can Eat

"All for one, and one for all." So say The Three Musketeers. "It's everyone for him/her self." So say customers about to attack and dismember eloquently prepared platters. It's buffet time. Abundant varieties of food attract hordes of customers. No limit on portions. "Fill up your plate, come back for more." Anything goes. No one keeps track of whose turn it is. That's poor buffet etiquette. Time comes when the food runs out. Buffet stragglers end up with slim pickings, planning to be first in line at the next serving.

Decaf or High Octane?

We drink decaf to banish the heebie jeebies. "Didn't sleep a wink last night. Must have been the coffee," says a yawning fireman. "Slept like a log. I drink decaf," replies his buddy from hook and ladder. Arguments rage between those straight coffee drinkers and the decaffers. Straights—"'Bug off. Stop polluting our coffee. Your stuff tastes awful." Decaffers—"Healthful. Wholesome. Only Juan Valdez can tell the difference between straight and decaf." To settle matters, we asked Pamela Grinder of the Coffee Bean Institute. Swiftly she replied, "Decaf is on the way out, killed by restaurant and diner owners. Order decaf and you wait tons of time until served (a new pot is brewing). Order straight, it's at your table before you can say Chuck Full of Nuts." Pamela Grinder offers this prospect. "Consider decaf an endangered species. Drink coffee straight with some heebie jeebies."

Fortune Cookies

On a remote Midwest campus, a building stands dedicated to the finest goals of learning scholarship, integrity, intellect. That building houses the School of Fortune Cookie Writing. Student body, averaging 500 a year, is made up of achievers the world over. Many who have an affinity to the subject matter come from Asia and the Orient. Degrees are granted for successfully completing work in one of the major departments, whose names roughly correspond to the cookie messages. (1) Department of Health, headed by Dean Kimmell, M.D. (2) Department of Business, headed by Dean Alladin, CPA, Emeritus. (3) Department of Hard Knocks, headed by Dean Flatbed, top union negotiator for Fortune 500s. (4) Department of Surprises, Dean Melton heads up this group. Former standup comic, he inserts surprise fortunes into the unsuspecting cookies. School President, Zong, addresses each writing class to establish the proper tone. "Customers who crack open your fortune cookie want to read exciting news about great events waiting. Don't disappoint. Make them millionaires. Send them to Hollywood. Cure diseases. Assure future cruises. Sprinkle your prose with holidays and vacations." President Zong concludes that the school is offering an MA and PhD program in Fortune Cookie Writing. Cheers and applause! Confucius say, "it is not uncommon to add "in bed" at the end of the fortune when reading it aloud."

Is Breakfast The MOST Important Meal of the Day?

Nutritionists advise that breakfast is the key meal of the day. It's a fast starter and a quick picker upper. But how many agree? Surveys show that most would rather skip breakfast and make the most of lunch or brunch, a meal eaten late in the morning, combining breakfast and luncheon items. Let us examine what gives breakfast such a bad reputation. We can gain insight from Biff Breakstone, a first meal of the day booster. "The menu is eater unfriendly. The S word is often used. I love the stuff, but who else does?" Cereals, Cereals, Cereals. Here comes the server to lay it on. You won't hear many yums yums or watering mouths. Wheateena, Oat Meal, Brans, Special K, Krispies, Crunchies, Toasted Muffins, Nuts. And that famous cholesterol triad, bacon, sausages, and scrambled egg yokes. Breakstone calls for greater variety and attractive looking dishes. "Blend colors into a work of art. Food that looks good will taste good!" Biff Breakstone forecasts, with enthusiasm, "BREAKFAST WILL BE THE COMEBACK KID!"

Make The Most Of
a Smorgasbord

Four friends are seated in Nora's cafe with calculating looks. Ron, the CPA, has figured it out. "Bud, you pile it on thick at the all-you-can-eat smorgasbord counter. Return and we divide the booty." As Bud takes notes on food preferences; Ron is a big tomato man, Jeb raises the ethics question. To no avail, he is outvoted 3 to 1. Ron's Plan. While Bud is harvesting food, appear independent to reduce suspicions that something is fishy. Consume the order of toast with relish and gusto that even on-lookers envy. Plan B. Push the food aside when the server passes, probably not necessary if Plan A is followed. No use taking chances of discovery. Plan C. Wait for distractions to fetch deserts, every man for himself. Server drops plates; wedding party enters or departs; two tables heartily sing happy birthday to you. Plan D. Folding napkins neatly in place, each of the party beats a gradual withdrawal to the exit, smiling at the attractive cashier. Finally, Bud follows reading the check with furrowed brow.

Now You See It;
Now You Don't

Now you see it; now you don't. This is a magician's familiar tease as he performs slight of hand, deception, trickery, and hocus pocus before a rapt audience. You will find this sort of legerdemain where you dine. (Now you see it.) Waiters scoop up hardly finished entrees and carry plates back to the kitchen. (Now you don't.) How can you protect? A party that has suffered onslaughts names a designated watcher. Her main function: guard the food, at all costs, against premature removal. At an adjacent table, strategy is clear. Everyone sits tight, no movement until the meal is completed. Constant pleas, "May I remove this or that?" are greeted with resounding "No's!" Weddings create some special problems. Six-course dinner. Strike up the band. Dancing. But when you return to your table, the barely-eaten course has disappeared. You rise to Cha Cha Cha, fun and frolic. Forget about the barely-touched course no. 2; that's gone. At weddings you learn that: If you want to dance, you don't eat; if you want to eat, you don't dance.

Stain Removers

The magazine EAT NEAT reveals a problem from cover to cover. EMBARRASSING? But now that the facts are known, the answer is to solve the problem. Most of us are sloppy eaters. We leave as much food on clothes we wear as on the plate. Shirts, skirts, and blazers receive a large share of these decorations. Kind words come from the disgusted, "Not to worry. The stained garment is on the way to the washing machine." An aggrieved says that doesn't make sense. Use a stain remover. "I'll handle it with that new product that performs miracles, INSTAGON." In just minutes, the stain vanishes. Why? The injured are slow eaters whose minds wander. In this state anything can happen and usually does. Case studies from the magazine show that it takes these folks two weeks to finish breakfast. Other meals take longer. They hardly realize that droppings found their way onto the vest and trousers. Discovery occurs at day's end when plans are made to clean up the situation.

The Days When Airlines Served Food

Sandy loves airline food. She developed the taste at an early age, an army brat traveling with her parents all over the world. When she sits in first class, the menu is Filet of Sole Amandine and Chicken Kiev. In economy, fish and chicken. No difference to Sandy, she eats anything. Company visiting Sandy knows what to expect. A ride to the airport cafe where they dine on airline food surplus, leftovers from all flights. Sandy has privileges in airline cabins. Attendants raise her tray, lean back her seat, and tuck a pillow under her head. They and pilots up front realize a happy Sandy brings in more business. She can hardly wait to host Thanksgiving dinner and the Passover Seder. The centerpiece for both is a sleek model of the Concorde, ready for takeoff. Her airport shopping yields a fabulous turkey carryout with trimmings. The Passover Seder challenges. Undaunted, she relies on the airline special diet department. They create a table that even Moses would be proud to join. So…next time you fly, think of Sandy.

Who Pays the Check?

Dinner with friends at a restaurant. Who pays the check? Split it? Who can figure out how much each of the sixteen diners owes? And who can remember who ordered what? Some say, "Waiter!" Try her and listen to what you get—a befuddled account of what took place at your table. So, who pays the check? All turn to Sidney—he holds the best job, makes the most money. Larry works at a miserable job and makes the least money. Yet he asks for the check. And he receives it. Who finally pays? Claude. His rich uncle died and left him a fortune!

Boardwalks

Everyday Life

Air Conditioning

Are you an "I can't live without air conditioning" consumer? Although most effective during dog days, does your penchant for cool and cold apply to all seasons? If you conform, an outline of symptoms and activities seems in order. You have made sure that wherever you are, so is the air conditioning. Your home or apartment; car, bus, or train; buildings in which you work or visit; homes of acquaintances; theaters, restaurants, department stores. It is well known that persons without air conditioning need not invite you. A typical day: Making it through with air conditioning. Safe at home, apartment. Coolness pervades. Elevator transports to garage, both with A.C. Start ignition and cool air pushes out full blast. Leisurely ride downtown into cool building garage and up to office suite, extremely cold but no complaints. Lunch in building next door with access by an air conditioned cat walk. Quitting—reverse process. Please note that at no time did the air conditioner lover have his nose out in the muggy humidity.

Approximater or Preciser?

Ask Gerard for the time? "About 11:30." Ask how he's feeling? "Not bad." Ask how many attended the meeting? "Around six or seven." Ask if the meeting was successful? "More or less." Gerard is very detail-challenged. Many are. They live their lives in general. It is difficult to elicit straight answers from them. Are they born that way or is it an environmental factor? No one knows. Gerard and his ilk also dress approximately. Clean but wrinkled shirt, left collar buttoned down—right, undone; severe narrow tie with knot barely completed; display handkerchief top pocket of jacket, half visible, half tucked in. Pity Gerard and company when they come face to face with their opposite number, the Preciser. Victor, for example. Precisers don't deal with "abouts" and "arounds." They are cut-through-slush specialists, perhaps somewhat sharp but ready to take on timewasters. Recall Gerard's 11:30? Preciser's, 11:36. Gerard's meeting report, six or seven attended; four is the Preciser's figure, "Gerard arrived late." Meeting successful? Exceeded expectations, goal oriented. Dapper Victor, aroma of his cologne wafting through the air, departs. Tell the truth. Are you an Approximater or a Preciser?

Are You a Close Caller or Make Surer?

Are you a Close Caller or a Make Surer? If you call them close, you barely arrive on time, usually to the stares of anxious Awaiters. Reasons and excuses run the gamut. Awaiters have heard those wrongs before. "Traffic was brutal." "Never witnessed such a bad accident." "My dentist had to handle an emergency." "The kids' school bus got lost; new driver." Tardiness is tempered with understanding. Awaiters know your record and have come to expect split second entrances whenever you are scheduled to appear. You seldom disappoint. With Make Surers, nail biting days are over. They will get you to the church, airport, train station, and Uncle Reginald's on time. Their caution in that regard is often ridiculed. Within a family circle, the youngest daughter forecasts Dad's recommended departure time. "Dad, the plane takes off at 3 o'clock. Why do we have to be there at 11?" The question generates his often-told tale on how he had two hours to spare at London's Heathrow and missed the plane. "You know you can't be too careful these days." Spoken as a true Make Surer.

Avoiding A Speeding Ticket

Maria, I just met a girl named Maria…A Leonard Bernstein classic from *West Side Story*. Carefree and twinkly, I am belting out Maria, driving down the turnpike until distracted by a siren. A huge state trooper, at least six feet six inches, basketball player height, asks for a window roll down and advances the following data. "Sir, you were driving 60 in a posted 50 mile per hour zone. I clocked you. Have you anything to say?" I reply, "My odometer read 50." He says, "Fix it. Follow me." Fifteen minutes later we pull up at a rustic looking house used as a backdrop in Class B movies, prefaced by a sign in front, "Justice of the Peace," Jocko Wingate. We gather in his chambers, a kitchen with uncleared dishes. Justice Wingate moves them to one side to allow space for deliberations. I soon hear his verdict. "You exceeded the speed limit by ten miles. Fine, $60." I plea bargain for time, devoid of cash and checks. The justice and trooper smile. We will send you a bill. And do they! Next morning, it comes special by Federal Express. I buy time, bringing my attorney, Joel, into the picture for how the legal world looks at this. Here's how: "Pay them the $60 dollars." Maria, say it soft and it's almost like praying…"

Bank Business

When bank doors swing open, the interior primes for business and commerce. Staff line up at strategic places. Tellers head for cash drawers. There, they prepare for Paying and Receiving and counting currency ad infinitum. Safe unlockers, in a private alcove, check the rolodex for box owners and the authenticity of their signatures. Administrators sit at side desks where they absorb the big picture. Security guards obstruct the normal traffic flow, casting jaundiced eyes at nothing in particular. BUSINESS AND COMMERCE spring into action in form of the customers. Complainers are grouped together and sent to desk folks absorbing the big picture. A strange breed, these complainers. The bank is their sanctuary to gripe about any subject. Regulars understand why the longest queue belongs to one teller, who let's call Malcolm. An award winner at financial conventions, his change prowess is in the Gluiness Book of records. Thus, it stands to reason that customers needing relief from bills and coins of the largest dimensions, they position themselves at Malcolm's window for reliable, swift service. Reassuring for all concerned, the entry of Brinks guards, guns drawn. Also a signal that Bank doors will soon close.

Boardwalks

A boardwalk is a sidewalk with wooden planks. It supports as many events and activities as you find on the midway. The boardwalk population comes and goes, disappears and reappears. There are walkers, of course, as solos, duets, trios, quartets—all boardwalk regulars. There are as many activities as on the midway. Probably more customers, too. They line up for franks and fries, frozen custard, bumper cars, Ferris wheels, side shows, thrill-and-chill rides, photo machines, and sketch artists. And all these are located on one block! Most boardwalks face beaches, but they don't like each other. Kids spring up, spreading sand and dirt on the boards. Their hijinks give boardwalks a bad name. The ideal time to enjoy boardwalk life is when the kids are in school and the weather is cool. The worst time, although most festive, is during the holidays. Noise, bumping, swirls, and gridlock. Rolling chairs and bicycles cannot move. No place to go. Truly a still life.

How Do You Interpret a Calendar?

The calendar reminds of special days to observe. Some do, some don't. And some just don't care. Let's run down a few days for you to judge how and where you stand. New Year's Day. Hats, streamers, noisemakers. Midnight waiting. Hugs and drinks. Late to bed. Hangover. Are you in that picture? Presidents Day. Without their approval, our country's father and emancipator are merged into one birthday. Traditionalists like me squawk. Keep them separate. They deserve it. Which side do you support? Saint Patrick's Day. No difference. Wear the green on this day and everyone is Irish. Bars and pubs are the sites to celebrate the patron saint of Ireland. Green beer flows in unlimited amounts. If you exceed capacity, duck outside to watch the parade. Columbus Day. Many dismiss this day. "Not worth the effort. Lately Christopher has gotten a bad name. That king and queen deserve the credit. They put up the money." There you have it. Americana by way of the calendar. Enjoy!

Idle Chitchat

Barbers, beauticians, and dentists talk to you in the midst of the noise they make when using the tools of their trade. Shavers on your head for haircuts and trims. Blow dryers for styling. Drills for fillings, bites, and crowns. Overall, their discourse earns high marks. They mix up dialogue with news, gems, jokes, complaints, and an excerpt or two from an old Hollywood musical. Most chair occupants endure, but have problems answering questions. This upsets the operator. How can I respond, since I couldn't understand a thing above the racket? But answers are expected. In the chair: Your job is to convince that you're hanging onto every word using these signals—hand-clapping, foot-stomping, shoulder-shrugging, finger-exercising. The louder and more forceful, the better. After the chair: This is tricky. Stand tall, smile and say, "Ah ha," and leave the premises immediately.

Life in Circles

When you think about it, most of us live life in circles. There are the family circles, workmen circles, friendship circles, traffic circles, and on a plane awaiting its turn at the airport. Round and round we go and where we stop who knows? Those who planned future destinies had a hard time mapping out guideposts and directions. Without hesitation they decided that whoever gets lost or stuck, let them go around it. Thus, the circles as we know them were born. Consider then, the next time you are circling you could have taken a more direct route if the founding circleteers didn't take the easy way out. Alas, alack. Make the most it. Blend into traffic at the posted speed limit. Hoist a flag or pennant to show that you are an enthusiastic twirler. Resume a steady speed as you prepare yourself for the next circle that awaits right around the bend.

Pauses and Interruptions

Pauses and interruptions are facts of life. Seldom does a day pass that we do not face a situation that calls for patience and savvy to restore balance and to gain control. Up high in the friendly sky you await a landing at your local airport, feeling refreshed after two weeks in Barbados. You wait. You wait. Then the calm voice pilot declares, "Gate 15 has a 747 ready to vacate. We are next. Only a few minutes." Your plane circles. It circles, and it circles. Looking out at the scenery, you see reruns of buildings and shrubbery. Finally, an hour later, the landing. Some pauses are only a few minutes, others much longer. You phone a busy person at your own risk. It's worse when you urgently need information that only the busy can provide. You begin with a mild request to speak to Ms. Busy. Her secretary politely responds, "Please let me put you on hold. It shouldn't be too long." As you are glued to the receiver, the secretary efficiently asks if you are still there. You are and plead. It shouldn't be too long. Thirty minutes later comes the devastating news, Ms. Busy left the office. Please call again tomorrow. All things considered, shouldn't there be a better way?

Surname Unusuals

Surname unusuals have an edge over the rest of us. They expect and receive special treatment because their names warrant it. Unusuals play their role to the hilt, reminding all who they are and what they stand for. You are in the midst of an unusual when you witness him making a dramatic entrance, wearing odd-looking clothes to fit the name. Meet Arturo Bull. He works in public relations and feels thankful for a surname that conveys agility and strength. Arturo Bull wears a colorful matador cape. He often concludes a sentence with *OLE*. Enter Guy Wilde, named after Uncle Oscar. No poet. No writer. Guy prefers the high life, wine, women, the name, and song.

The Woes of Waiting

Twenty-two shoppers were recently interviewed at a sprawling mall. A question put to them: In life, what do you find most objectionable? Surprisingly, all had the same answers. It was "having to wait." I spend more time at the dentist's waiting room than I do in his chair. Likewise, laboratories where they draw blood and give injections! How do you cope with the waiting game? "It takes too much out of me," say some. Relax and make the most of the experience!

What are Windbags?

Windbags are non-stop talkers, out of control. Give them the floor and they will exceed their allotted time, filling in with repetition and difficult-to-fathom anecdotes. They should, but windbags never tune in on their audience. They ignore signs of discontent. Coughs and throat clearings and constant references to wristwatches are windbag warnings that go unheeded. In more restless surroundings, a listener, unable to absorb more, throws hands side-to-side, signifying, "ENOUGH ALREADY," but the drone continues. According to those who know, the issue is simple. Non-stop talkers love to hear their voices in abundance. Conversely, they make lousy listeners.

What is a Bad Hair Day?

A new wrinkle has been added to the nation's vocabulary: BAD HAIR DAY. What does it mean? And whom does it affect? What are the causes? When a person suffers bad hair day, their hair goes out of control. They avoid being seen in public. Efforts to remedy the situation usually fail. It is hopeless to employ an arsenal of cosmetics. The causes include (1) static electricity, (2) humidity, (3) rain and snow, (4) hats and caps. And a fidgety hair stylist. ANSWER: if you face this dilemma, your best bet is to hide or move out of the country.

What is on a Bumper Sticker?

A bumper sticker proudly proclaims, MY SON IS AN HONOR STUDENT AT PEAR HIGH SCHOOL. Beaming parents! Their child is rising up the ladder of success. Other parents may feel somewhat put out. Their children are slipping down the ladder, rung by rung, bit by bit. Then a time arrives; bumper sticker parents face reality. Billy flunks geometry, French, and gym. His average dips, his honors become tainted. Easy way out. Continue showing the bumper sticker. Hardly anyone will know the difference. But both Billy and parents are not deceivers. They are ready to peel off the honors. But hold on! Let's consider a new set of stickers with words to cover most students. For example: My child tries harder at Pear High School… My son is stuck with C's at Pear…Not to worry. My daughter is a choir singer at Pear…My son is a workaholic at Pear…My daughter is an almost honor student at Pear…My daughter will make or break it at Pear…My daughter didn't make it at Pear; transferred to Apple High School.

What to do With Snorers?

Snorers are public disturbers number one. No difference where they are. They make their presence known—loud and clear. But, how do you cope when in the path of a snore storm? You and 200 others are seated in a darkened theater following the exploits of James Bond of 007 fame. Nearby a snorer disrupts the action and breaks the mood. Sentiment: "Let's pick him up and throw him out the back alley." A more humane alternative catches on. "Tell him he's wanted on the phone. When he leaves, bar the door and pile clothing on his seat."

Where Could You go to Smooch?

During our tender years, smooching venues were hard to find. Scarcity of sites did not seem to restrict the process and the overwhelming numbers who participated. Tunnels of Love did a brisk business. Couples lined up to await entry into boats that slowly sailed in the dark to the opposite end. Total elapsed time for smooching—twenty minutes. Theaters were also smooch possibilities.

Advocates hadn't the foggiest idea what was playing, nor did they care.

Where to Hang Your Coat?

Ever notice that after entering a dining area, you cast around for a place to hang your coat? No luck. Some explore nearby rooms. Perhaps the architect has designed a special retreat for wardrobes. You know what happens next: commandeer an available chair for pile-on purposes. Less desirable, drape coats and jackets around your chair. The question remains: Why do accommodating places eschew coat trees and hangers en masse? An interview with a maitre d' hotel provides some clues. "We got rid of hangers because they created a giant headache. Coats look alike, so patrons took home the wrong ones. We had lawsuits on our hands. As a safety measure, the fanciest places in town have ripped out their coat-hanging facilities." Will the hanger trend affect other service areas? Exhausted shoppers look for chairs and lounges to rest weary legs. No luck. They scatter to furniture and beds for respite. If the trend continues, can park benches be far behind?

Who Replenishes Bathroom Supplies?

Replenishing bathroom supplies is a serious business. Heavy users cause dwindling and complaints. The Charmins, the Ivorys, the Crests, the Estee Lauders, as well as washcloths, and towels. Some have longer lives than others. But run out of any of them and the users suffer the consequences. The annals of tourism are filled with stories of the embarrassed persons who were prisoners in the stalls, without a shred of paper to complete the process. Call for help? Save your breath. No one on the periphery wants to become involved. There is a way to gain relief and exit: Firmly knock on the neighboring stall. In return, expect an overhead missile-like roll, right in the breadbasket. Depart with a poker face. No one will be any wiser for your experience. All in the family bathrooms have a custodian, usually Mom, to clean and replace. The time comes when wash-basin soap wears down to its thinnest consistency. It seems impossible for anyone to suds up with barely a sliver. "But let's be frugal," says Dad. "If hotels can use this soap size, so can we." Water flowing from the spigot sounds as if it's saying, "What's going on?" Mom, God bless her, in the dark of the moonless night, tosses out the sliver and replaces it with a robust, aromatic Dove. Everyone notices but Dad.

Why So Much Clutter?

Why do so many households throughout the land suffer from clutter to the extreme? At any given time, they accumulate a wide range of goods, some of which are items in their possession since purchase or access. If owners do not demonstrate a willingness to reduce inventories they face an inevitable clutter. Here are the worst offenders and why. (1) Magazine subscribers. They save back issues and decorate walls and floors with them. Visitors can hardly make their way from room to room. To do so involves stepping on Life magazine and the New Yorker. The matter becomes serious at moving day. It takes a genius to pack up the clutter. It takes nerve to dispose of the unneeded.

Should Toddlers Sit in Grocery Carts?

Families - Babies, Kids, & Children

Baby Transports

You can't miss them. The many ways to carry or transport infants. Some are so ingenious that they defy detection if the little one really exists. Strap-ons, knap-sack style, seem trendy with the younger set. The baby can view scenery in front or rear, depending on the carrier's preference. But as baby matures and becomes heavier, strap-ons must give way to other conveyances. Baskets are ideal for to and fro—from car to cafe; from home to park; from uncle to aunt. In the cycle, baby outgrows the basket and is ready for a *stroller.* Parents who do not want to relinquish cuddling assume long-term carrying responsibilities that terminate with shoulder strain and back aches. A time soon arrives when the stroller occupant is visibly restless and impatient, rattling the side frames. *He wants out!* He signals, *Carrying and transport days are over.* They are. He begins to walk.

Carry on the Family Name

Plumbers, plumbers, plumbers. Doctors, doctors, doctors. CPAs, CPAs, CPAs. Teachers, teachers, teachers. Here they come, the parade of workers and professionals led by Dad. The key question posed to youth, "What do you want to do when you grow up?" The reply: "The same thing that Dad does." In most instances, the youngster does not have freedom of choice. Mom and Dad call the shots with persuasive reasons that it is family tradition to continue lineage without interruption. When your reliable plumber answers a house call, notice the two young apprentice helpers he brings along, his sons. Signs outside a doctor's office are all in the family surnames. Dad exclaims that just like continuing a family name, it is important to continue sort of a family business. What do you want to do when you grow up? Call Dad.

Family Names

Parkinson Wyat believes in family. You know the type. Ask a simple background question, then prepare yourself for a family tree discourse dating back to the first twig. Wyat has family facts that intrigue listeners. For instance, he claims that his ancestor, Lathrope Wyat, sailed with Columbus as first mate. Parkinson and his wife, Stephanie Wyat, made sure that the family name would continue generation to generation. The firstborn and those who followed are Parkinson Wyat I, Parkinson Wyat II, Parkinson Wyat III, Parkinson Wyat, IV, Parkinson Wyat V, and up to VIII. Only a mother knows. We asked Mrs. Stephanie Wyat a pointed question. "What happens say around the breakfast table? Except for you, father and sons all have the same names. Doesn't this create an identity problem?" She chuckled, then became serious, realizing my viewpoint was probably shared by others. "You see names are out, it's the numbers we go by. As Parkinson Wyat III joins us late we greet him, 'Good morning III.' Then IV chimes in, 'Had a rough night?' 'None of your business,' says the talkative II. You see we are a speed calling family. You don't have to dial the exchange. Press the number, you are connected. Say the number, and you have a Parkinson Wyat."

Making Faces

Observing is believing. Place adults in the company of children and they become transfixed. They make faces to reflect the awe of the occasion. Range of faces depends on age and cuteness. Infants and babies seem to have a lock on the market. Tots with braided hair and pink ribbons come in for a share of attention. Look around you when the next adoring opportunity occurs and match faces with the following: ADMIRING FACE. A quick count reveals that this is the one most used. But don't expect duplicates. Some admirers display sparkling eyes while others wide smiles. A longing expression has a vast following. BABY FACE. Obviously, the adopters wish they were young again. The more successful resemble and make baby talk, hoping for approval of anyone listening. Two or more baby faces lead to clashes and arguments. I was here first. PUFFY CHEEK FACE. Close your mouth tightly. Then blow until cheeks expand. You have puffed cheeks and ready to show off. Approach target carefully because your face may scare and be greeted with a chorus of loud cries. EYE POPPING FACE. Favored by those whose features already show popping characteristics. A lift of the brows and the eyes stand out. In the adoring group are also SQUINTY EYES FACE, WRINKLE NOSE FACE, AND TONGUE OUT FACE.

Rearing Children

Rearing children has its starts and stops. Children just can't wait to learn and apply themselves immediately. Family members assume new roles such as becoming a "bike steadier." Your eight-year-old tries to balance on a two wheeler. She hobbles and wobbles while you run after her to prevent tips, slips, and falls. She becomes adept at age ten. Scene changes to the world of peer pressure. "My friends drive cars, why can't I?" From "bike steadier" you become "driving instructor." Worrisome? Not as much as when her license arrives, declaring you have a bona fide driver in the household. That first night when she drives the family car, solo. Frayed nerves until you hear the key in the front door. Rearing children has its starts and stops. Is it worth it? Scene changes. The bicycle rider and motorist you nurtured is the CEO of a top Fortune 500 company.

Shopping for Baby Gifts

Shopping for baby gifts can pose problems. What to buy? Will your choice please the recipient? "You can always return it," no longer strikes a responsive chord. "Why don't they get it right at the start?" a comment from a designated returner. At the Outfit Your Tot store, merchandise gets a good going over. A shopper emerges with strong preferences. Clothes and other wearables. Keep away from toys and teddy bears. Store clerk brings forth a parade of adorables. Smiles. Size depends on the baby's age. Not to this strong-minded old wave shopper. "The larger the better, allow the baby to grow into it." A Federal Express truck pulls up in front of Baby Hannah's house. Driver, balancing five gift boxes, gains entry t an excited audience. Mom and Dad split open the boxes, crediting the senders. Hannah stares. (1) "Lovely pajamas from Aunt Ellen," says Mom. "You can put four Hannahs into them," says Dad. (2) "Perfect booties from Crocket," says Dad. "But I would say a size smaller than ten would fit Hannah a lot better." (3) Friend Ginger Rogers gives Hannah tap dance shoes, the same ones in which she learned how to dance. Mom drafts thank you notes; Dad dials dance teacher, Ray Wasser, to register Hannah for advanced beginning tap lessons.

Should Toddlers Sit in Grocery Carts?

Toddlers in food carts attract and distract. Attract? Shoppers favor the little ones. They make funny faces, talk to them and offer a toy or two to show their ffection. Those nearby march their kids right up to the toddler, an experience in bonding with the young. Distract? You better believe it. In the cart the toddler performs certain antics that only a toddler can perform. He hurls overboard most items that parents selected and stored on the way to checking out. He hums and whines unrecognizable tunes, he insists on having a Coke, Pepsi, or Sprite, the drinking of which results in a stained shirt from the overflow. Toddlers in a cart make sense when you consider the alternatives.

What is the Answer to Childcare?

Working parents must plan on a childcare center if both wish to continue at their jobs. It's a decision most take seriously. The hunt provides training for later years when the student and Mom and Dad seeks out colleges near, far, and farther. You check out credentials for the Center that fit your son's or daughter's needs. Locatio? Curriculum? Staff? Facilities? The day arrives for the first day of school. Everyone experiences tension. Expect the youngster to act up, wanting to remain and play with toys. You soothe feelings on the way to the car, moving toward The First Step Child Care Center. A problem! Do you turn right on Spruce or left on Oak? No difference. You're lost. A friendly gas station attendant straightens you out. Finally you are there at First Step and greeted warmly by Mrs. Fiji presenting you a rose and a coloring book for son, Booker.

Who do you Want to Be?

Kids are often asked, "Who do you want to be like when you grow up?" Responses surprise. (1) Notary public with a red rubber stamp. (2) Tonto. (3) Boris Yeltsin. (4) Joan of Arc. (5) Traffic flagman who guides drivers on the road. 6) Superman, Batman, Wonder Woman. The number one wannabe of past years, no longer interests the kids: PRESIDENT OF THE UNITED STATES.

Why Cylinder Shaped Boxes?

As kids we looked forward to Moms emptying those cylinder-shaped boxes that contained pot cheese, always purchased in bulk. Couldn't wait. We accelerated the process by consuming more cheese than the others. Why? An empty cylinder meant a crude but reliable talking box with the guy across the yard. Punch a hole at the cylinder's base, insert a waxed string that has sufficient "reach ability," punch another hole in a like cylinder and there you have it: a speaker and receiver. It worked! The yard's landscape had as many waxed strings as clotheslines. Moms in conversation wondered why their kids were so crazy over pot cheese. They didn't suspect that their kids were pioneers in high tech. Listen in, you would find that some of the talk burned up the wax. Dates were a popular and favorite item. Male: "Were you able to break down her resistance?" Answer: "She said she wanted more time." Female: "Does he come across as good as he looks?" Answer: "He said he wanted more time." Living life through cylinders. Lines are clear. No busy signals, no party lines and area codes. Straight talk, one on one.

What is Videonucleosis?

Medical

Broken Appointments

It seems that appointments are made just to be broken. Case studies tell us why. Drawn from the magazine *No Shows And Why,* the issue is put in perspective. A critical set of factors emerges from appointments with doctors. Potential patients cancel for a variety of reasons. Fear tops the list. "What I don't know, won't hurt me. What I do know, may." This thought runs through the mind of Cora Kissick as she dials Dr. Chicago to cancel a podiatry appointment. Meanwhile in an adjoining office, "Cardiology Mary" reschedules twenty-three appointments to fit in emergencies. Concession: Mary offers free dinners at Howard Johnsons to the dispossessed. During these hectic times appointer and appointee maintain calm to preserve stability. Few complain. "It's the American way to wait your turn. That's what made the country great," says Bert Townsend with obvious skin blemishes, spending time in his dermatologist's waiting room. The NO SHOW magazine preaches civility. "Broken appointments is a two-way street. Reschedule with dignity and respect. A flash of humor relieves tension and demonstrates good will."

Diplomas on the Walls

Do you feel more secure in a health or legal provider's office to see a bevy of framed diplomas, certificates, and complimentary letters glowing from the wall? As you eye the display, do your innards tell you: "Dr. Billings has the right stuff." OR after a diploma digesting period, you conclude the opposite, "Dr. Billings has a huge ego." "Next, the doctor will see you now." In the examining room you come down on the side of ego, especially when Billings reviews his academic triumphs and seminar successes. It doesn't help listening to his reading of letters declaring him "the best and the brightest." You depart amicably but with a lesson learned. Next time you want a provider who has DIPLOMALESS WALLS.

What Body Part is Next?

Recovering from touch-and-go surgery, the doctor says, "Go home, rejoice, and take it easy." But before becoming Joyful, you hear voices from within—your other body are parts piping up. "We are miffed that your gall bladder received all the attention. You'll be hearing from us soon!" True to their word, Joyful's ear begins to ache. Then a bite into soft food splits a bridge in three places. Waiting in the dentist's chair, Joyful experiences a sharp pain in her left foot. Next stop, Podiatrist Consuelo. The skin has been yet to be heard from to settle the score, but suddenly, emerging from Joyful's face is every blemish known to dermatology. Is relief in sight? Not as long as Joyful's back acts up. Resourceful as she is, Joyful turns to her first love, writing. "REVENGE OF THE BODY PARTS," by Joyful Salvo.

What is Phlegm?

Phlegm drives people nuts—night, day, and when they are away. It is the mucous that lives deep in the throat and torments its host in unusual ways.

1. It clogs. This results in a big build-up that blocks nasal and breathing passages.

2. The Ahems. Sufferers must clear their throats often, no matter when, where, and how. The most discreet method used is ahems. It blends into conversations and provides a modicum of intellect and respectability.

3. The spits These phlegmatics have had too much and won't take any more. They release the accumulation, at times embarrassingly, in public places. Witnesses, not realizing that this is an emergency, use such words as "uncouth," "bum," and "homeless," which is unfortunate.

4. The medication. Doctors prescribe pills to reduce the onslaught. Taking them consistently, some relief occurs. But one side effect has consequences: a complete dryness of the throat and the complete loss of the voice. Ask a pharmacist? Reply: the old phlegm wins again.

What is Videonucleosis?

Videonucleosis. This is the term the behavior specialist used to describe an associate who was acting strange. He talks back and argues with his television set. Before presenting a treatment or cure, a little background. I first became aware of the problem when I invited my associate to dinner, during which I switched on Geraldo. He stood and marched up to the TV, shouting, "That's what you say! You're wrong! Who do you think you are?" I grabbed him before he could phone the station and put a gin and tonic in his hand. Later spoke to his wife. She said it started five years ago. A dog-food commercial ticked him off. "Says who!" he screamed at the announcer. The cute dog barked, did nothing to soothe. "Expected," opined the behavior specialist. My treatment for Videonucleosis is quick and sure. Defuse the shouter by booking him live on shows that upset him the most. My patients have enjoyed fame and fortune on the stage, TV, and movies. Winners of Tonys, Emmys, and five Oscar nominations. A perfect channeling of frustration for fun and profit.

What to do in Waiting Rooms?

On the surface, waiting rooms have few advocates. The more modern rooms have agreeable decor, average reading material, playgrounds for the young, and reams of records, one of which is yours. Enter a waiting room and you become a census taker. You count how many will precede you before your name is called. Spying a chair close to the receptionist, you establish an operating base to survey the "preceders." As one departs, you keep a mental record of who is next. What gives? Three newcomers appear; no waiting, in they go. Murmurs and unrest until behind the desk, Rhea assures "These are emergencies." You wait. After all it is a waiting room. The numbers dwindle and it is your call, finally. As you walk, you analyze: (I) Subtract the number of waiting folks; some are impostor who frequent offices "just to sit around." (2) wear a cap or hat, logos preferred, to make a statement of presence, and (3) cultivate staff and technicians speaking to them on a first name basis.

Pets & Other Animals

New Zodiac Signs

According to the Chinese zodiac. Buddha summoned all the animals; those who came had a year named for them. Each animal gave traits to persons born in its year. Headliners on table mats: Year of the Pig. Year of the Rooster. Year of the Dragon. Year of the Monkey. Standing by are Dog. Ram. Ox. Hare. Serpent. Horse. Rat. Tiger. Milton Castor, an ardent fan of Chinese cuisine, furrows his brows, takes exception. His doodles transform the icons into grotesque figures. Rat sprouts horns. Ox takes on a rider. Dragon takes a wife. Milt signals or the manager and provides him with a new approach to zodiacism, illustrations and headings, (1) A quill stands for the year of the lousy handwriting. (2) A TV stands for the year of lousy programming.(3) A hamburger depicts the year of inferior airline food. (4) Franklin 100 dollar bill reminds all of the year of high price tags. Manager shares Castor's creativity with a table enjoying a dinner for ten. Milton Castor and the table for ten receive double order of egg rolls and especially prepared fortune cookies for service.

Pet Audience

Animal owners often lineup their charges in front of TV sets toabsorb commercials. What they see is the narrator asking for comments from a nearby cat, dog, parrot, canary, and a gold fish swimming in a bowl. Each responds by extolling the virtues of the product in question. Meanwhile, the viewers gush with loud sounds of approval: barks, meows, chirp, chirp, chirp. Owners reflect on financial possibilities of training their pets for a career change. Sid Fein, agent to the (animal) stars, accepts the challenge: "Bring in pets tomorrow for an interview. But please leave the goldfish home."

Pets, The Loves of Our Life

Pets, God love them, provide owners with renewed spirit. They banish the sulks and the blahs. Depressions fade when a pet enters the picture. Note a grumpy owner. He scoops up a handful of his Fidos and Felines, and depression turns into exhilaration. The pet parade consists mainly of dogs, cats, parakeets, canaries, parrots, and for the more daring, snakes, slugs, and snails. Make no mistake about it, pet care and pet raising require skll and patience. You derive great satisfaction for the effort. Training. Forget about the "Give Me Your Paw Concept" and "Sit." These are old chestnuts. The most crucial now is for your pet to convey the urge for bodily functions. Relieves stress. Prevents a mess. Talk to the animals may do it. Pets like for you to walk them down the boulevard. They spy first aid stations: fire hydrants, trees, walls, gangling long legs. Obviously, training days are over! Prepare for blessed events. Why not take pride in additions to the family.

The Excitement of Zoos

Located in urban or rural areas, zoos dot the landscape. They are popular family fare as well as high on the list for school outings. A visit proves memorable in a tot's life, so much so that they will endlessly tell zoo stories to anyone who won't listen. Adults move into the zoo scne for photos. They want snapshots of favorite animals that possess telegenic qualities. Clusters of cameras surround jumping seals, monkeys, giraffes, tigers, and strutting peacocks. Visitors can derive the fullest benefits if they prepare. A map tells where you are and where you are going from entrance to exit. How can you tell that your visit has not achieved expectations? Count the number of times you stop a zoo guide and inquire where to find a building or an exhibit. If the stops total six, it shows marginal preparation.

Idle Chitchat

Situations & Events

Auctions

Going! Going! Gone! An auctioneer's chant that a Ming Dynasty vase has been sold to the highest bidder. Next lots: Oriental rug, six Hummel figurines, three-carat wedding ring, grandfather clock, silverware service for ten. It takes practice to attend an auction. Just walking in off the street may cost you time and money. Some houses use bidding signals: A face-scratching, earlobe-tugging, nose-blowing, shoulder-lifting, and mouth-yawning. The uninitiated who innocently resorts to one of these bodily movements can find he owns an original Van Gogh. What does Purvis Pratt think, author of *Auctions I Have Known?* "Dressing hippy, sloppy, or goofy is out. Dress to look like other bidders. A boutonniere for men and necklace for women add a stylish touch." Demeanor Pratt talks about first impressions. "Strive for a look of self-confidence. Show that you are a bidder to be reckoned with." Bidding if you are a first timer? Bid early to attract attention. Then settle back and allow others to carry on while you learn the ropes. It's best to mingle and mix. As you move toward the door, walk arm and arm with a fellow bidder and remark, "Wasn't that a spirited session?" Obtain name, address, and telephone number for future reference.

Bullies

Bully is a word that sends shivers up and down the spines of the abused, harassed, and the picked upon. The word conjures unpleasant memories when a disagreeable oaf struts up to your social circle, striking up a conversation on no subject in particular. If you ignore, he seeks new prospects. Mabel Carter captures the tone. "Once a bully, always a bully; they are born that way. Bullying is just part of their make-up." Some advice from Dr. Jordan Bethlehem. "Never argue with a bully. By so doing, you will acquire his worst traits. In other words, you become a bully and cast about for prospects of your own." Continues the doctor, "Relieve tension, treat the bully to a shrimp cocktail and a martini chaser to wash it down."

How To Deal With Restlessness?

A common attraction in public places is restlessness. You suffer from it and when you look about, you see fidgetites who just can't be still. They demonstrate jumpiness in a variety ways, all of which bother the many located nearby. (1) Exiteer clears the way passing his neighbor on the way toward the back doors. A half hour elapses, and a return trip is assured. (2) Exerciseer does all moves on her Jane Fonda tape, and she executes them with perfection. She uses the aisle to perform jumping jacks and jogging. (3) Neck stretcheer. Oftentimes this is done in place. The stretcher can be heard humming a tune to provide rhythm. A popular ditty: Toot, Toot, Tootsie. How do you overcome boredom? It's your move!

How to Dry Your Hands in a Public Restroom?

Drying hands in public places take the form of rough paper sheets that spit out of a dispenser or blowers that gush at the touch of a button. The soft tissues that double as nose blowers and, as standbys, the handy squeezable soft rolls are found in stalls. Which provides the best service? The answer depends on preference and the depth of wetness and also mechanical efficiency. Pulling down rough paper sheets are done with wet hands. Tears and splits in sheets result. You are left with a tattered sheet to dab and dry. Blowers are quirky. They should automatically cut off after a specified period. Some I have used droned on and on long after I vacated. Are they trustworthy? Not when they emit cold air, hardly the performance promised on the nozzle. Finally, soft tissues have their advantages. They are the quickest absorbers. Only minus in their use, it takes so many of them to complete the job. It makes a poor impression to clutter the sink with twenty to thirty softies.

Name Tags

Enter a meeting, party, seminar, and someone slaps you with a name tag. "Why?" "So everyone gets to know each other by name." "But my name is not Mars." "Oops, here's a magic marker. Fix it." Get to know each other by name? Looking around, it becomes clear that the tag names cannot be trusted. Try to ring up or become friends with the following, taken from name tags. LEG, TUNA, HUMP, TUBS, WART, DUNK, BENT, HUB, 36/24/30. Resist name tags. Tell the giver you just want to be yourself. And by the way I'm MARK, not Mars.

No Gift Policy

Good friends and close relatives disregard NO GIFTS prohibition on invitations. They consider it a blow, a shock for future relationships. They enter the premises laden with boxes, food, flowers, and deserts—seeking out the celebrants. Meanwhile, what do the no-gifts crowd do? A few depart immediately and head home to corral some trinkets stored for years in a closet. The more steadfast disregard the interlopers and socialize. For the dubious, a visit to No Gifts Inc. can yield results. They can obtain nothing at bargain prices. To signify the visit, they receive a certificate that they give to the host, indicating compliance with the spirit of the event.

Promises, Promises

Promises. Promises. Most everyone knows some person who means well but cannot deliver. Godfrey is such a person. No doubt that his abbreviated name, God, inspires confidence. "If He can't do it, no one else can," a remark heard after Godfrey agrees to tackle a tantalizing problem. His can-do lifestyle makes him the envy of the bashful and the timid, in fact anyone who is afraid to take risks. But can he deliver? Pearson Prosac doesn't think so. "Two years ago I expressed interest in a camera that gave you a print the instant after snapping. 'Hold on! I'll get you one tomorrow.' That was two years ago. I'm still waiting." Jocko Jackson had a similar experience with his recently published first book, *Comment and Dissent.* "Whoa Jocko, that calls for an autographing party. Order 500 copies, and I'll take care of the rest." "That was three years ago. Still waiting as 500 books gather dust." Bridget Van der Meer has some choice words about Godfrey. "His efforts as matchmaker made me nauseous. Singing 'Love is Just Around the Corner' he showed me photos of several potentials. Five years later love was stuck there. Godfrey, spin your undeliverable magic somewhere else. Matrimony is none of your business!"

The Boss is Retiring
- Who's Next?

The boss is retiring! In corridors, on all floors, deep in offices are sad, long faces, lumpy throats, misty eyes, streaky mascara. "What a guy. He spent time with us. He advised us, inspired us. He promoted us to better jobs. Who will take his place?" That question looms large as the key to the future. Successors. Do they measure up or do they measure down? A clue to their potential is management's recruiting skills. Facing an austere budget, personnel engage a rock bottom head hunting firm, Squeeze and Sleeze. S and S vouches for candidates with impeccable references and credentials and offers a six-month trial period. Meanwhile, he retired boss vacates his desk and admires his gold wrist watch, a gift tendered for thirty years of loyal service. Lurking in the background is the successor provided by S and S. He doesn't seem to make the grade. Packing and Shipping mark him down, strictly on personality. His outbursts, "How I'm doing" is confusing because he has not assumed the reigns of his position. Unanimous, the successor cuts a dramatic swath on coffee breaks. Staff finds this policy ingratiating. Talk among them that the successor is a regular guy.

The Wonders of Nostalgia

When it's time to talk vacation, one of the parties reminisces about returning to the place "where we had a fabulous time." Nostalgia. Will that place of fond memories be as fabulous the second time around? Car gassed up, hotel reservations in hand, we begin the journey to yesteryear to find out. First stop, our honeymoon hotel. Star struck, we approach with expectations and palpitations to again visit Room 436. SHOCKER. The site is a sight. No Shangri-La. Our love nest has become an unkempt parking lot. Next we repair to the horses and buggie. In those nostalgic days, Emile was our driver. He conducted a captivating tour of the city to the clop clop beat of the horses. We look for Emile. He's gone. Also gone are the horses and buggies. Jitneys are employed to do the job. The doors are open to Gem, our favorite restaurant. As we move closer, it is not a gem but junk jewelry. "Recall the tie store and that wonderful Mrs. Shelly. Let's see if they are still there." THEY ARE! We greet Mrs. Shelly and hug her. She remembers us, the honeymoon couple. We buy twenty ties.

Waiting

What do most of us simply dislike WAITING AROUND! We put in our share in the waiting game. Some familiar venues include online purchasing of tickets for entertainment! Movement depends on how brisk are the sales. The hospital takes its place where we spend countless hours. Take Goodman Metric. In a special room, set aside for these things, Goodman looks forward to the announcement of his Blessed Event. At the butcher shop, you have an orderly wait, with numbers in hand to move you ahead when yours is called! Perhaps the most trying wait is in the offices of medical personnel. The nurse assures that the doctor will be with you in a minute. HE NEVER QUITE SHOWS UP! While it lasts, enjoy your wait.

What is Fantasy, LTD.?

Fantasy, Ltd. has more business than it can handle. Phones ring incessantly; mail orders pile up; customers pound on the door; fax machines go nonstop. Why? What does Fantasy offer to achieve such notoriety? Its motto reveals intent and purpose: "We will make you over to the person you always wanted to be." The process intrigues because it is so simple. Candidate, Biff Hudson, tells the interviewer his preference is becoming a FIREMAN. Fantasy accepts the challenge by placing a fireman's hat on Biff's head. He is then given a notarized letter declaring him a fireman, eligible to join any fire in progress. Signatories: six fire chiefs emeritus. Nora Kane dreamed of having an operatic career. Fantasy understands she lacks talent, but quickly moves Nora to a higher level. She enters the Lip Sync laboratory, operated by voice coaches of world renown. Her ability to "voice over" most difficult passages astounds the faculty. Nora Kane is a contingency diva and performs in the chorus of the Metropolitan, La Scala, and the Baltimore Opera Co. Her next appearance will be in Carmen in Baltimore.

Where is the Light Switch?

Light switches are difficult to find in strange surroundings. A friend's house, restaurant, highway rest stop, theater, sports arena, or in the milroom. Hands move every which way to find the on/off and shed some light on the situation. Hotels are the switcher's biggest challenge—and the occupant's. Look upward and you will find the switch near the ceiling, or downward at the base of the floor. Giants and midgets are happy beneficiaries of this design, but they rarely patronize these hotels. The most grievous blunder is no switch at all, the overzealous work of a paperhanger. Graphics will solve the problems. Tack on a sign or decal next to the switch for best results.

Who is Invited?

Whom do we invite? This can become more daunting than the event itself. The issue doubles for weddings with a merging of lists from the bride's family and the groom's. Independently, the marriers swell the number of invitees by adding a generous chunk of their own. Meanwhile, pencil sharpeners cast around at lists and the event to provide cost effective data. This has a bearing on the extent of the effort. Planners sensing an unbridled build up Invokes "the immediate family" constraint. Acceptable, but for a few who haven't the slightest idea who constitutes the immediate family. Cousins confuse. In all families, so many exist and are spread out at all ends. "No problem," says the aunt matriarch. "Call Cousin Finders. They will find all of them, at $5 a cousin." In paring down the lists, an ultimate test is to eliminate persons who did not reply to earlier invitations or attend previous affairs.

Why Bother?

Have you ever thought about why people engage in certain practices that to you and others seem preposterous, or at the least entirely unnecessary? Standing in line for a dining room table, you receive a 3 x 5 card which is punched by an eager staffer placed there only for that purpose. Hours later you return home, empty pockets that include a blank, punched 3 x 5 card. WHY? The puncher's reply, "You can't take chances." In an office setting, another line, this one for picking up weekly salary checks. Behind a desk the disburser reuires that each recipient affix a signature on a lined pad. Sign and shine. WHY? "We have been doing it for years. Oh the signatures, we toss them out." Next, a busy publishing office where editors are proofreading for what they hope is the next bestseller. Curious. One editor reads from typed pages and the other follows from negatives. WHY? The typed pages have been cleaned up from a previous reading. The negatives reflect exactly content on the typed pages. "You never know. Negatives aren't perfect." Please pass the Tylenol.

What is a Memory?

Socializing

Are You a Joiner?

Who among us does not belong to a club, society, council, sorority, fraternity, or an assemblage of some kind? Very few. We are a country of Joiners. It's the American way. We take pride in togetherness. But as it must to all Joiners, they meet at the big one, THE ANNUAL CONVENTION. Goers fall into distinct categories. (1) Stay as long possible conventioneer. This Joiner lives for the moment, testing programs, facilities, resources, food, and drink. By sheer numbers, they dominate and create a budget-less environment. (2) Make way for Joiners who make convention attending an art form. They skip lectures, meetings, and related functions. But to their surprise they are greeted as active participants. They are recognized from the podium as Joiners with the most interest. How do they do it?

Are You a Waver?

America has become a nation of wavers. Think of it. You must share in that distinction. You wave because of friendliness. You wave because of avoidance. You wave out of habit. Neighbors are waver regulars. Indoors, they hardly set foot in each other's homes. Outdoors, they wave, they wave, they wave. In the Gresham Gardens condominiums, Benson Boxer is recognized as champion waver. He holds the record because after dinner he settles in on a chaise lounge and for two hours he waves to anyone or anything crossing his path. Friends, strangers, cars, taxis, cats, and dogs. To many, waving becomes a defense mechanism, a courteous signal to those you wish to avoid, "Hello and Good-bye." Recipients of this type of wave get the message. Don't be upset if you do not see a wave in return. Finally, the habit wavers can best be described by Jason Pelican. He has waving in his genes. Proof of the tendency? He finds streets deserted during a morning constitutional. Jason knocks on doors, says hi, and waves.

Bar Regulars

Bar flies, regulars at the nation's watering holes, are standard fixtures, morning, noon, and night. They are a pleasant lot. Whiling away the hours, drinking on the rocks and straight with a twist. The male contingent focuses on office matters, a Hollywood star, or a son of a bitch who lives next door. Females, make no mistake about it, feel completely liberated in the bar setting. No holding back, forceful conversation. The ladies give as well as take. Then, walking through the entrance comes a non-regular. Heads swing from side to side, throats clear, drink orders fall off. Even the jukebox malfunctions. It's up to the bartender, an expert on assimilation. This time he feels music and song the answer. After drawing a beer for the stranger, the bartender breaks out with "Irish Eyes," "Old Mill Stream," "You Made Me Love You." The bar becomes a chorus. Discomfort disappears.

Challenges Of Dating

Dating is a prelude to affairs of the heart. Like the first round in the ring, participants size up each other, reveal strategies, and prepare to make a go of it. On a date, two agree with the idea that they should meet and do something together. Look for daters at these familiar venues: restaurants, movies, theaters, museums, cruises, churches, synagogues, and bicycle and hiking paths. Dating oftentimes fails because the two parties don't prepare, leading to bumbling and stumbling. Lars and Tanya could have made a go of it. Signs indicated a romantic link. Both were ill prepared. In conversation, Lars was unable to form a simple declarative sentence, much less his affections. Tanya's trouble? She had difficulty remembering that her date was Lars. Not Mars, Bars, or Cars. A brief encounter with friend, Wescott, a jokester, relieved tension. Lars and Tanya scheduled a date for the following Saturday with an inward vow not to take anything for granted. (Five years have passed. Lars and Tanya are happily married, parents of five children.)

Class Reunions

Class reunions. The high school variety, I avoid, mostly for bias reasons. I am, however, fed a steady diet of reunion data by the kids' groovy Dad, by friends who after ten years still converse in high school lingo, and the four-color invitations that shimmers about that fateful night. Again I don't attend, but listen to my qualms quotient. Calm for reunions held within ten years after graduation. Fidgety for reunions that hit the twenty-year mark. The mirror test raises concerns, "If I look like that, they all will." Irreconcilable, the thirty-year reunion. Charades! Few recognize each other. Scrambled names; Is it Teara, Toora, Tara? Chuck, Chit, Chet? Aria, Aora, Aurora? The fanfare. Most Likely To Succeed, Bat Lytel, graces the stage somewhat embarrassed. All reunionees know that Bat did not climb the heights. Works as a shipping clerk for Bloomingdales. Nevertheless, a thunderous ovation.

Convertible Owners

Owners of convertibles must adhere to some sort of code: after you buy the car, make sure you have a steady stream of regular passengers, family, relatives, friends, and a stranger or two. No matter who, convertibles need a full complement with the wind and the rain in their hair. Owner Brad Sylvester adheres, looking chirpy as he drives the Interstate and expounds on the fine points of his convertible. But are his passengers as chirpy? Judge. Brad picks up Aunt Hester at the beauty salon after a three hour stint with her hair stylist. She smiles as the car gains speed, laughing on the outside but dying on the inside. Aunt Hester's hairdo is obviously hair done. Hypochondriac Willie is along for the ride, following doctor's orders. "Don't fight it, Willie. Enjoy the scenery and fellow passengers." But not for long. Brad makes an unscheduled stop and dumps Willie at a Roy Rogers. Ride resumes but Brad Sylvester realizes these passengers do not have convertible qualities. He pulls into a Baskin Robbins, "the cones are on me," and cuts the trip short, pondering a new list of passengers for the next ride.

Cruising

The band on the second deck reminds passengers "Happy Days Are Here Again." A cruise is dedicated to making it so. More lively music and good fellowship. Some jigging and good-bye waves to friends and relatives below. Prior to "All ashore who are going ashore" tearful embraces. Why? It's only a three-day cruise. The returning passenger can beat the tearfuls home if construction blocks road traffic. As the ship slowly glides out to sea, officers and crew conduct a life jacket drill. Many just cannot get the hang of the ties, knots, bows, and stretches. Gastronomy, the hidden passenger agenda, now comes to the fore. Deck talk from stem to stern, "Will the cruise food live up to its reputation?" Doesn't take long to find out. A sumptuous dinner awaits one and all in the dining room. Complete satisfaction. It becomes obvious from this sampling who on board are the professional eaters; they have a stomach capacity for six meals a day. On a cruise, by darting in and out of dining rooms and on-deck barbecues, that can be easily accomplished. For late night hunger pangs, the midnight buffet. Relaxing on deck, you meet the entertainers who you will see again later in the ballroom. A gabby shipmate tells that some are heading for Broadway or Hollywood while others are destined in the other direction. Happy Days, but the cruise ends, returning to the departure dock. Excitement prevails. I pack away my returning home outfit, especially the pants, in the suitcase that, with a hundred others, makes its way to the ship's hull. Somewhat flustered, I pass through customs in a long, battered raincoat.

Do You Suffer From an Inferiority Complex?

Inferiority Complex was a term bandied about several years ago. Who had one? Who knows? But without a shred of proof, a free for all occurred to designate certain members of society as having an inferiority complex. You were so designated if you displayed the following tendencies: (1) shy, (2) timid, (3) bashful, (4) withdrawn, (5) unable to hold forth in social situations. From the pain of these unfortunates, a cottage industry emerged to return them to the mainstream. "I'm now a success," boasts Dexter Wexler. Make friends easily and influence people; should have heeded Dale Carnegie's advice years ago.

Is There a Psychic in the House?

A staple of boardwalk strollers is the fortuneteller, known as a psychic. Her patrons travel from afar to determine destinies. Quite a few come from off the boards, some clutching rabbits' feet and wearing good luck charms. It is easy to spot the fortune teller. Unlike her business neighbors, she believes in colorful displays, visible from long distances. Locations include store fronts and especially designed tents with futuristic motifs. An audience with a fortuneteller costs a few bucks to defray expenses. Image is important to create an aura of mystery. The teller might wear a turban, the teller might talk to a lighted globe, the teller might toss around cards, exhibiting pained and pleasant expressions, precursors of the fortune yet to come. "Good news! Your future prospects are bright." You hug Madame Kay, slip her an appreciated gratuity, and return for a brisk stroll on the boardwalk, heading for the frozen custard stand.

Key to the City

Picture this. Downtown cleared for a ceremony. Flags, bunting, high school bands tuning up. The air permeates excitement because the mayor, with police escort, will greet famous dignitary on the first stop of his American tour. THE YEAR— 2010. To swell the crowd, offices and schools shut down, encouraging one and all to attend. Siren wails, crowd cheers. Principals are in view. STRIKE UP THE BANDS. Mayor escorts dignitary to most favored chair on platform. He says, "Start cheering, let the ceremony begin." OOM PAH PAH, OOM PAH PAH. Bass drums signal the crowd that this is something special. Then the mayor introduces and presents the dignitary a token of affection: the key to the city. Recalling that the year is 2010, crowd sends forth approval roars. The key, they know, is a 2 x 3 inch, white plastic card with puched holes, the kind used for hotel rooms in 1995. A parade ensues, lasting four hours. On the sidelines, vendors busily are selling duplicate city keys for $5.00 a pair.

What is a Memory?

Revisiting old haunts that provided earlier fun and satisfaction is a dicey proposition. Several key factors emerge. The destination, the date, the recollections, and the persons who contributed to your having "the time of your life." Considering alternatives, a popular choice for the second time around in places you enjoyed when you were young. Here, the nostalgia bug bites hard. Dates. Roller Coaster. Dances. Ocean Beach. Boardwalk. Hot Dogs. Frozen Custard. You know where to go, what to do. Fun waits. Or does it? What's wrong? The people. They are not friendly. What's happened to my old friends, David, Stanley, Lilly, and Kermit with his funny jokes? They're gone, and so is the feeling that you can live the old times again. Memories. Memories.

Sports & Recreation

Hear The Grunts

Tennis spectators and TV watchers hear a medley of grunts as players serve, return, and address the ball. Aficionado comments explain that the noises are sound effects to accompany strenuous strokes. "Wrong," says Bruce Deuce, foremost tennis authority and winner of four grand slams. "Coaches include grunts as part of training to unnerve opponents. At crucial stages, a certain kind of grunt can provide points necessary to win a match." The magazine, *Tennis Anyone?* features a weekly series on grunts. An old standby, strongly recommended, a surprise grunt an octave above normal speaking voice. Expresses an emotion, "Should have made that one." Brings in the crowd favoring the missed shot grunter. Much lower on the voice register is the guttural grunt signifying frustration and disgust. Crowds dislike this grunt, some even boo. Poor sport. Bruce Deuce advises tennis watchers, "Enjoy the matches, and keep your ears open for these grunts."

Observation From the Lifeguard's Perch

Pool lifeguards observe a variety of shenanigans from high up on their perches. Their main job is to save the distressed, but they can hardly overlook the obsessed. Dana Bates, hall of famer, tells the magazine, *Water Follies*, just what goes on. SUBMERGERS sink to the lowest depths to test how long they can hold their breaths. Dana Bates cuts through the water on a rescue mission. He signals to the anxious, "No drowning. Just another damn fool." SPLASHERS aim salvos at whoever happens to be in range. Their sprays result in swift lifeguard intervention. Security takes over and escorts the offenders into the locker room. PETS out for swim. "It's raining cats and dogs," shouts a pool regular. Lifeguard toots whistle to attract master's attention; pets respond by doing tricks. Security takes over with nets that snare animals and master, moving the quarry to the local zoo. TIMIDS fear water and stick to themselves. Easily identifiable, they wear inflatable tubes in the jacuzzi and hover at the two foot level. Heading for the pool? So am I. Last one in is a rotten egg!

Pool Temperature

Some who first step into a swimming pool have problems adjusting to the water temperature. Although reassuring, signs declare "You have entered a heated pool," Shiverers need convincing. "No way is the water warm," says Thomas Doubting. Along poolside, a lifeguard shouts, "Move around, you'll get used to it." Thomas shouts in return, "I want to get used to it BEFORE I go in. Now, not later." This calls for a lifeguard meeting with maintenance. Thermometers are dropped into the waters confirming that frigidity does exist. A call goes out for boiling water. Scores of teakettles spring into action and are brought to the pool. Their contents do the job. Lifeguards keep a wary eye on swimmers checking degrees at frequent intervals.

The Attraction Of Beaches

Trekking the dark tunnel from hotel to beach, you contemplate fun and frolic. Forget family and office woes. Ocean breezes further lift spirits as you settle behind the lifeguard. Why take chances? It's time to unwind. Your eyes pan like a camera the surroundings. The exercisers demonstrate agility, standing on each other's shoulders. To the left, two lovey doveys grab attention. Everyone understands DO NOT DISTURB. Suddenly! A floating volley ball game, right on your turf. You become a ball retriever. Just as suddenly, players move to another field. The bathing suit underclothes crowd arrives. No middleman, no bathhouse. Clothes off, ready for splashes. Time for a dip. Note that the waves have tidal tendencies. Run in? Back off? The skies open with a steady rain. That is the beach signal to scatter and run. Heading back to the hotel tunnel, you see complete evacuation. One exception: the lovey doveys lie unmoved. TNT could not budge them.

What Happens in Locker Rooms?

Locker rooms are the last refuge of the sexes. Men are men and women are women. Their inhibitions must be checked at the doors. Locker roomers gab a lot. Men exchange views on sports, women, cars, and manage a sprinkling of off-color jokes. Ladies' chatter consists of diet, weight, recipes, gossip, children, Bloomingdales. The big question looms, "To dress or not to dress." The shy and bashful suffering from exposure problems, curl in corners and head for exits. Meanwhile mainstreamers strip, put on shorts, bathing suits, sneakers, then store gear in the lockers. With passing hours, affection grows. Activist, Sid Pipps, seizes the occasion by announcing all present are charter members of a new club, The Prime Time Locker Roomers…Word spreads to the women's venue. Good and welfare. The shy and bashful take heart. They are led to mental therapy sessions after which they join mainstreamers. Renewed timidity results in a one-month suspension in locker-room activities. Signs point to confidence-building.

What is Stickball?

As youngsters growing up in the hustle and bustle of New York City life, we played on the streets a game called stickball. The bat (stick) consisted of the wooden end of a broom or mop. The ball was usually rubber. The bases were sewer tops. For competition, we chose up sides. Players were infielders, outfielders, pitcher, and catcher. No umpires. Closest to the action made the call. Seated on foding chairs, neighbors made up the crowd. They viewed stickball with disdain. Referred to us as wild Indians. Perhaps their sour dispositions can be measured by the number of windows our hardy batters managed to break. It should be noted that quite a few players became famous doctors, lawyers, and high-level government officials. Candidates for sensitive positions were subject to background security checks. One of our players was being considered for the Supreme Court when it came to the fore that he was really a wild Indian.

Why Marathons?

Physical fitness buffs dream marathon whatever they do, stretch walk, or following a celebrity's exercise tape. Marathon, marathon, marathon. What makes these buffs think they are capable of running twenty-six miles, non-stop, to qualify, much less survive the rigors of a marathon? Sheer confidence. "I want to win the big prize," says a housewife during an interview in the midst of Jane Fonda's jumping jack session. Revealing are the fortunes and destinies of some of the buffs who join multitudes to compete. (1) Lost. It takes the edge off of winning and breaking a record. Marathon follows a circuitous route. Jane Fonda can hardly prepare the misdirected who end up in strange surroundings. (2) Cook Outs. Yards included in the route are sites of picnics and barbeques. Runners join up and partake in the special servings. They feel that they can make up for lost time. (3) Hitching a Ride. When runners become car passengers, they violate the rules of the road. They pay the price, but are awarded a medal as the first contestant that won in a motorized vehicle.

Your Coach

TV fans witness sufferers and, oh, how do they suffer! They are college coaches. Plenty of agony, but little ecstasy. They show pain when the opposing team scores because of blunders and miscues when their charges cannot quite put it all together, and when the referee makes the "wrong" call. Different types of anguish. (1) There is the running up and down coach. It doesn't take much to excite him. Even if the time clock is off by a second, you see outbreaks of bellicosity, and running, running, and running. (2) There is the flailing, I-can't-believe-it coach. The whirling dervish of the sidelines, his players are in harm's way if they stand too close to him. (3) And there is the fall-to-the-knees coach. He reserves this tactic for close contests and overtime to disarm the referee. But does it work? Leaving the arena, the referee is nimble, skips a step or two, and hums a Bruce Springsteen tune. In contrast, leaving the arena, the begging coach hobbles, leaning on a cane to steady his wounded knees.

Travel &
Transportation

America's Love For Automobiles

America's romance with the automobile is storied and legendary. Old time magazines show drivers with goggles behind the wheel of early cars of the period. As time goes by, new models strike the public's fancy. Trade-ins, upgrading, sales, and purchases. These transactions lead to the car of record, one that the owner will drive, show off, and maintain with every ounce of strength. Car maintainers are serious and resourceful. Self taught (no school offers courses), they are day/night laborers. Their visual acumen is wondrous. From a top floor of a high rise, they can spy dirt, dust, and spots attacking their vehicle. Call for action. The avid maintainer loses little time. He's on the scene—bucket, brushes, rags in hand—washing, cleaning, and shining. For the neighbors, he knows that the car he drives home must look as good as the car he drove to work. They notice. Regrettably, most do not possess car maintenance genes. Those who do can share their zeal with us less fortunate and adopt a car or two as if it were their own.

Amtrak

Those of you who want to travel along Amtrak's east coast corridor, prepare yourself for The Big Shake. You reverberate as the train squeals, squeaks, and rumbles. Under these conditions, adjustment must become a way of life. For instance, drinking liquid refreshment poses a problem when the water, coffee, tea, milk, or soup jumps over the rim with each bump, staining your traveling attire. Stow away reading material and stationery. Bobbing heads and shaky hands interrupt focus. Write a letter while the train is in motion and you will have trouble recognizing your own handwriting, much less the message. Finally, the big challenge on the trip is making your way to the restroom, usually located quite a distance from where you are seated. As you "ease" down the aisle, holding on becomes a necessity—the overhead luggage shelf, other passengers' seats, a conductor's shoulder, anything you can grab. Finally, you are in the restroom. Hardly. The noisy, screeching, rackety train doesn't help with natural functions. A passenger advises new travelers: "Wait until the train slows before a station. I do all my business in Wilmington."

Exit Only?

Road mavens try to develop signs to keep traffic moving in the right direction. Arrows also come in for their share of display. Then there are warnings: NO LEFT TURN. NO RIGHT TURN. NO U TURN. DO NOT ENTER. ONE WAY. THRU WAY. NO WAY. But perhaps the most ingenuous of these devices is ONLY. It creeps up on you when you least expect it. Then you're stuck in a long line with genuine ONLYS and run the risk of missing a crucial meeting. How do you extricate from this dilemma? God ONLY knows!

Hate Potholes

Potholes....POP POP POP. SHAKE SHAKE SHAKE, BANG BANG BANG. ROCK AND ROLL. What to do? It seems that potholes follow you wherever you go. Loose tire rims, forget about alignment. Driving becomes an obstacle course. Best solution: Tolerate the worst for thirty days, then check out the damage at your local garage. Send the bill to the road department. IT'S THEIR FAULT!

Hotel Dilemma

When registering at a hotel it is wise to check out the refurbishing and painting schedule. A manager who proudly announces, "We have done the place over" is suspect. Of course, you respond with expressions of approval, but ask for more details. Also make sure that you are not given the room last painted. This assignment gives a beaming manager great satisfaction, but has a certain amount of risks. After a night on the town, a couple returned to the hotel room with friends to review the day and preview tomorrow. A few drinks and it's time for good-byes. But no easy exit. The door is painted shut. Their only access to the outside is door banging and phone calls to the desk. Trapped by paint, couples are reassured that they will be freed in no time. "To us this is routine." ROUTINE?? Three hours later, during which late-night movies have run their course. Shouts beyond the door warn to stay clear. Bang, chop, the fire department to the rescue. In relating the story to me, I did not hear any traces of anger. "To be frank, we had fun. And I saw my favorite movie twice, *Dawn Patrol*."

House of Cars

In the neighborhood it is called the car house. Every occupant for over a decade (and there have been many) has had a love affair with a car. It began with Ben, the head of the family, that first moved in. Morning, noon, and night he spent more time with his Cadillac than with his family. Ben was a washer, shampooing the Caddy to perfection. Then came Jerry, more of an under-the-hood man. Engine tune-ups, plug replacements. Oil changes, battery charges, hose checks, on and on and on. Skipping through time, 23 Becker Lane is the proud residence of a Korean family all dedicated to cars. They own five foreign makes that are in tip-top shape. If we can imagine a parade of cars at some future time, my neighbor across street leading the pack.

How Are Streets Named?

A new city is born. Planners talk it up. We want something special. A place that's the tops. Tourists will visit in droves to stay and to spend. A solid name attracts. Let's try Mount Ethno because street names will follow along ethnic lines. Nestled in a sleepy hollow bordering an interstate, Mount Ethno makes TV talk shows, covers of prominent magazines. And editorials in the New York Times and the Christian Science Monitor. Founding fathers and mothers busy themselves figuring ethnic street names, the signature of the city of Mount Ethno. Disagreements ensue but the final tally is unanimous. "The main thoroughfare, running through the center of the city. ROSENTHAL BOULEVARD. Feeding in are side streets SCHWARTZ, KAHN, NEEDLEMAN. Mount Ethno has scores of traffic circles that the founders set aside names beginning with letters C and K. An easy to remember device. Thus COHEN CIRCLE, KELLEY CIRCLE, and KATZ CIRCLE. For traffic are feed ins and run one-way. An enclave consisting of malls dominate Mount ETHNO suburbs. Shoppers hustle there for sales and bargains at Acropolis Avenue, Athenia Parkway, Shish Kebob Junction, riding the Maria Callas Metro. Also prominent on street maps: Venice River, Placido Plaza, Pizza Park, and Antonio Freeway. You can't mistake Mount Ethno citizens. They have pride written all over their faces.

How Do You Go Through Customs?

The returning overseas traveler tenses up at the prospect of having to face customs. Agents differ in approach and technique, all identifiable in uniform and badges of authority. Customs are crap shoots! Methodical processing? Swift processing? It depends. On you, on the agent, and where you have been. They won't confess, but some custom agents envy. Look for body English and facial expressions. I understand. That is why I soften the hurt and dress up for the customs experience. I have learned that snappy dressers are respected by the customs contingent and admired by those waiting in line. It creates an atmosphere of rapid stamping of clearance and waivers for those behind you. It is refreshing to witness such a speedy beeline toward the door.

Hurry Up And Wait

What's the rush? Time to get to work! Time to get home! Those respondents move behind the wheel, setting off a chain of events that commuters abhor the world over, RUSH HOURS. To and fro, drivers blend into swelling traffic as a number of vehicles join the lanes through specified entrances. In a matter of minutes—10, 15, 20, 30, and above, a standstill. In the language of the road, bumper to bumper, gridlock, snarl, snafu. Why the delay? Rush hour drivers can't tell, but hunches prevail. "An accident up ahead." "A goofy cyclist ran off the road." "A cop is misdirecting traffic." "Just one of those days." During the holdup, many leave their cars to become acquainted. Naturally, the topic of talk is the delay and estimates of how long. Rush hour breezes reveal other exchanges: What is your name? Where do you live? House or Apartment? Where do you work? What do you do? Any family? Then, of all things, comes a job offer. Looking for someone, want a job? Before saying he sure does, the roar of the motors, the cheers of the crowd. Bad break. Traffic moves. Rush hour blues.

Snowbirds

In regions of the country most frigid, many gather to plan the GREAT ESCAPE. They waste little time in making their way to the warmest climate. Resorts expect the influx, cautioning staff, "Take good care of THE SNOW BIRDS." These special guests receive treatments most special. They are escorted away from drafts. They swim in heated pools. They are wrapped in special blankets to reduce the chill. A SNOW BIRD ritual is to keep tabs of back home temperature and to cheer at the news that those who they left behind are freezing their butts off. SNOW BIRDS frequent food-friendly restaurants that recognize their status with generous portions, refills, and discounts. But it all comes to an end when a cold snap causes the thermometer to equal that at home. Fond memories and a foundation to DO IT AGAIN NEXT YEAR most positively.

The Allure of Museums

Museums. Sooner or later a call is heard within the family circle, "Let's all go to the museum." Usually advanced on Sunday when the suggester reads rave reviews of a traveling art exhibit that began in Paris. It is time for cultural cleansing, far surpassing concerts, lectures, seminars. Also, less expensive. Preparations begin. What to wear? When to go? Invite friends, family. Take a side trip afterwards. Eat out, eat in. Finally, at the gallery it becomes evident that the family is not art aficionados. Far from it. The telltale sign: a tour guide advises that one can achieve a deep perspective by looking at a painting with one closed eye. Chaos! Two eyes shut. And Picasso, Renoir, Cézanne, and company bear the brunt.

The Color of School Buses

At a recent PTA meeting, an innocent exchange on student transportation turned into a brouhaha, and of all things, about the color of school buses. Kim Kerchief, madame president, proudly announced purchase of six more buses to add to the fleet and to relieve congestion. Serge Silo, parent of two first graders, roared his approval and said, "This time let's buy yellow buses." Hannah Footen, veteran substitute teacher, gasped in disbelief. "Mr. Silo, with all due respect, all our buses are a bright canary yellow. What color do you make them to be?" "Orange." "Gold," says Ingrid Rubin, student counselor. "Bronze," chimes in Candy Carlson, who holds the attendance record for consecutive PTA meetings even though her progenies are grown and attending college. Finally, "dirty, that's the color." Arguments, loud talk. President Kerchief slips out to phone bus driver, Dan, to join the meeting and settle the issue. He arrives at her beck and call. President Kerchief: "Dan, what is the color of our school buses?" The reply, "Don't ask me, Mrs. Kerchief. I'M COLOR BLIND!"

The Orient Express

The train departs from Victoria Station, London, bedecked and bejeweled. Passengers in the diner, club car, and compartments prepare for a once in a lifetime journey on THE VENICE SIMPLON ORIENT EXPRESS. To gain insight, I rent the movie, Murder on the Orient Express. What suspense! And I feel I'm a prestigious passenger. Dress means everything. They DRESS TO THE HILT. I check off a suggested wardrobe as dictated by an Orient Express veteran. Monsieur: A mustache is a must. Grow one, paste it on. But don't leave London without one. Dress shirt, colored light magenta with matching ruby cufflinks. Try open neck, but carry a snap-on bow tie if formality takes over. A designer Burberry three piece will make a statement of balance and style. A cape, loose and swaggering, silver buckle shoes, qualify you as a passenger in the highest standing on THE VENICE SIMPLON ORIENT EXPRESS. Madame: Bracelets. Bracelets. Bracelets. Necklaces. Necklaces. Necklaces. Jewels. Jewels. Jewels. Long, sleek, clinging skirt. A matching long hanging knit sweater. Shoes, high heels and pointed toes with cameo buckles. All is rounded out with cigarette holder measuring ten inches. And French manicured fingernails. At first serving for breakfast, we share a table with two French teachers. Good conversations, they are beguiled by the brown, paste-on mustache. It wins out over bracelets and jewelry. Next day, Orient Express shock. At the same table, mustache-less we are not recognized. Under breath is overheard, "they have some nerve."

Too Little Space

The tall and the gangling have problems in fitting into chairs, taxis, cars, trains, and planes. On closer examination t seems that builders of resting devices provide adequate space for bodies of below average dimensions but not for those who need the most room to maneuver. Warning to whoever feels squished. Beware of the taxi experience. Hail cabs at your own risk. (I) You can barely get into the space around entry doors. (2) You can barely sit in the rear seat. Why? THE DRIVER HAS PUSHED BACK HIS SEAT FOR HIS COMFORT. Complaints result in disagreeable episodes. Only recourse is to reduce the amount of tip commensurate with your aggravation.

Trolley Cars

In our youth, some of us loved railroad trains, especially the ones with steam engines. It's an impression that can last a lifetime. When you see that iron horse barreling down the track and hear that "choo choo" warning to step aside, it's indeed an awesome sight. A vanishing transport mode but still popular, is the street car. Desire of Nw Orleans fame has made the archives as America's national trolley. Then there is that red truck for the few, but needed by many, the fire engine. Who hasn't wanted to ride in one and, admit it, to become a fire person? Now to the Midway. Pick and choose. Dare devils settle on the roller coaster, tuning up yells and shrieks. The more sedate occupy Ferris wheel compartments, slow and easy with a panorama view of the countryside. But why jangle nerves and stomach. Take a boat ride, cool and collected, through the tunnel of love.

Turnpike Rest Stops

Turnpike planners carve out lines and signs for us to reach destinations. Lines, good; signs, questionable. An historian is probably the father of rest stop signs. Designations include James Fennimore Cooper, Woodrow Wilson, Joyce Kilmer, Molly Pitcher, Clara Barton, and others. Then it may not be too farfetched to hear this conversaton. "Ready to stop? Let's drop in on the Coopers. They have everything we need." "But the Wilsons are so close. Like to see their 14-point dishes." "Or the Kilmer's newly completed arboretum. We might get some free cuttings." But with due respect to our writers and statesmen, shouldn't these gas, eat, make and go stops be identified with more familiar personages. Donahue's Run and Stop; Geraldo's Gourmet; Make It at Montel; Rock with Rivers; Leno's Lounges. If it is just hamburgers, try Dave. My apologies to Woodrow and Joyce.

Vanity Plates

You can't miss them. Car license plates on which the owner advertises his or her name, a message, a peeve, or hat have you. What's the purpose? Vanity. Mystery. I.D. Must have some serious intent because those special plates cost a few dollars more than the standards. Let's review some pedestrian and traffic showstoppers to judge whether value is received. TUNA JIM. What do you think? Either a fishing enthusiast or a constant fan of the blue plate special. GA GA GA. Difficult to decipher without explanation. Ecstasy. Love. Indigestion. A dieter's or receptionist's credo. And KLUTZ, a commentary of what the car owner thinks of society.

What is the Importance of the Asterisk?

The asterisk is the traveler's worst enemy. In print and on TV, these star-like symbols attach themselves to words and phrases that convey "please look below for omitted material." Many who follow the asterisk trail end up in a state of shock. Mickey and Myra Katz are innocent examples of confusion and befuddlement. In the Times travel section, they drooled at the ad of spending a week in the Bahamas for 75 dollars, air, hotel, food, and entertainment included plus a stack of quarters for the slots. Exhilarated, the Katz's departed from JFK for a dream vacation. In their excitement, however, they failed to read the asterisk. Sad experiences for Mickey and Myra. Hotel Winston Churchill ran out of rooms. Manager, Henry the Eighth, read them the asterisk, "subject to availability." He set up two cots in Housekeeping. Another Blow: The maître d' refused to seat the Katz's. He whipped out the asterisk that stated reservations are required for the dining room. To tide them over, the Katz's carried out grilled cheese sandwiches to eat on the cots. At check out, they were relieved that the 75 dollar rate prevailed, gladly paying it for outstanding services rendered.

What is the Reality of Moving?

Only a dunce looks forward to moving, according to Valentine Majestic, a veteran of at least nine dislocations. With his traumatic experiences, he cannot fathom the whys and wherefores coming from "those dunces who haven't any idea what moving involves. Packing. Join me as I sort out five years worth of possessions, which my wife and kids call junk. JUNK, how dare them! My books, awards, diplomas, paintings, prints, letters, caps, gowns, wall clock, knick-knacks, and a photograph personally autographed by Spiro Agnew. How dare anyone to ask me to separate these accumulations." ULTIMATUM. "We don't have space for your collectables in our new home." Give them away, sell them, and get rid of them, options that send pain into a broken heart. At considerable expense, storage becomes the solution. Nearby a warehouse offers a moving special. The outdoor sign says, "We will take care of your goods so that you won't have to throw them away." SOLD. I deliver all my stuff, but retain the Spiro Agnew photo for historical purposes.

Where is my Luggage?

Ask any traveler about luggage at the airport and you will receive the same answer: CONFUSION! The stories are filled with a variety of details. LOST heads the list. This forced owners to spread around in search of their luggage. A further factor is seeing some stranger carrying the luggage as if it was his own.

Who Reads Maps?

Reading maps can drive you nuts. What's the problem? The map is the problem! It takes a special skill to unravel, translate, understand, and interpret. What troubles the user are wiggly lines, asterisks, and arrows pointing in different directions. A steady diet of fathoms in the Atlantic Ocean and Great Lakes obscures the main purpose of getting there. Latitudes, longitudes, and attitudes confuse. A designated map-reader eases tension, enabling the lost to be found. Unfolding and then folding maps requires patience of the highest order.

Why Do We Crave Adventures?

It is difficult to understand how the shy and timid early in life become high risk, devil ma care, anything goes adventurers as time goes by. A parent muses over the issue. A cricket had more nerve than my Casper. So how come he's going to Africa on a Safari?" Another parent faces roller blade madness, currently running wild, "My Tiffany, docile, demur, and distracted. Can't believe she won the roller blade derby in Atlantic City." The twins never wanted to travel and visit. Now their pictures are plastered all over the Times society pages at the homes of the rich and famous. They must take after their father's side.

Why do we Migrate?

We planet earth inhabitants are constantly on the go. You are in bad form when you become a standstill. You may be looked upon as a lazy and a do nothing. What else can critics say; swifties pass them and they see you, left at the gate. "Should we shake him and get him moving?" the critics' consensus. Standstill stands still no more. In a pincer action, he finds himself in a pedestrian flow with directions where to move on. MIGRATE, a word that promises a better life and future. Humans do it. Ducks and geese do it. A wide variety of fish do it. Animals in jungles, deserts, in cities, and on farms do it. Humans make moves in stages, bits at a time or huge areas, to reach their final goals. European immigrants who came to our shores are examples of the hardies traveling thousand of miles, seeking a good life.

Weather

Do We Believe The Forecasters?

Do weather forecasters become despondent when they misfire? Are there morning-after blues for predicting sunny, gorgeous? Outside they see a deluge; wind buffeting lawn chairs, trash cans, and Nicky's three-wheeler. Our fearless TV forecaster gathers data from near and far. On neatly drafted maps he shows highs, lows, and some Alberta clippers thrown in. Based on the data, viewers decide what to wear. The deluge! Explanation: Highs were sidetracked, the Clipper detoured, but we are still looking for the lows. Please phone this station if you see any.

Temperature Control

You can bear witness. Place several persons in an enclosure and listen to them sound of: "It's too cold in here." "It's too warm." "Turn up the heat." "It's drafty." "It's stifling." Few seem to agree on what constitutes the ideal room temperature. Spouses raise the issue as a primary bone of contention. Bedroom blankets become frayed because of constant tugging to gain advantage. Matters become severe with seasonal changes. Somewhat higher Fahrenheit signals heat-cutoffs in public places. Spring and summer are a long way off, but the thermostat regulators herald their arrival. Complain, and you are greeted by resort talk. Accept the situation and enjoy the movie wearing an overcoat. "It will be warm when the theater fills." It never does. The issue takes on sharp edges in cars where passengers realize that the designated driver controls their destiny. Since in a carpool, each has a turn at the wheel, it pays to move the thermostat *quid pro quo.* The world of entertainment has reached a crossroads. Patrons on a night out hardly consider artists or the program. They attend on the basis of the temperature in the theater. TWO THUMBS UP!

Retirement Party

Anniversary Party Celebration

CPSIA information can be obtained
at www.ICGtesting.com
Printed in the USA
JSHW010249310523
42401JS00004B/19

9 781947 939431